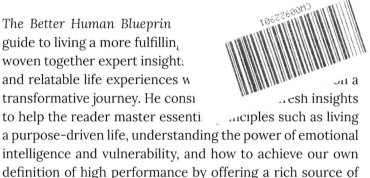

The Better Human Blueprin
guide to living a more fulfillin﹐
woven together expert insight﹐
and relatable life experiences w   ⌐ a
transformative journey. He consi   ⌐esh insights
to help the reader master essenti   ⌐.iciples such as living
a purpose-driven life, understanding the power of emotional
intelligence and vulnerability, and how to achieve our own
definition of high performance by offering a rich source of
diverse and inclusive suggestions.

What sets this book apart is the relentless focus on the
ability to take and apply the principles immediately. This is
more than a book you'll simply read; I'm confident it's a guide
you'll love. Don't just read about change – embrace it and
embark on the journey to becoming a better human today.

**Professor Damian Hughes – international speaker and
bestselling author**

There is much truth in *The Better Human Blueprint* and a real
opportunity to engage with it in a thoughtful and constructive manner. Deep down we all ought to know how much
inclusivity matters, not as some theoretical concept, but
actually in day-to-day life. It doesn't matter much if it is in
the classroom, on the sports field or at work, being excluded
is horrible, and being included provides camaraderie and
teamwork and is ultimately more productive. None of that
should be rocket science but it still needs to be reinforced
and too many of us need reminding.

Caroline Nokes MP

I've learnt that you can't effectively lead people or an organisation without first having the knowledge and skills to lead yourself. *The Better Human Blueprint* delivers this knowledge in a way that's approachable, easy to digest and relatable. It's a carefully researched book with stories and references that helps you form your own opinions. Importantly it gives you the persuasive vocabulary and insight you need to communicate why you feel and act as you do.

Simeon Quarrie - founder, Vivida, Google mentor and UK Creative Entrepreneur of the Year 2024

Throughout my corporate career in leadership roles and playing in various sports teams, I have learned the importance of self-leadership as the foundation for leading others. Achieving excellence requires not just skill but a deep understanding of oneself.

For busy professionals, this book is a game-changer. It saves you the time and effort of reading countless development books by distilling key themes and highlighting the most important insights. Pete Cooper has done the heavy lifting, presenting the core concepts of personal and professional development in a concise and actionable manner, and highlighting where to look next.

The practical applications are profound. The book provides actionable insights that readers can implement in their daily lives, whether in the workplace or in personal interactions. The outcomes of applying the principles outlined are transformative, equipping readers to lead themselves and others more effectively.

The Better Human Blueprint is a remarkable resource for anyone seeking to enhance their leadership capabilities and personal growth. I highly recommend this book to young professionals committed to becoming better leaders and better human beings.

Nick Welby – vice president of England Hockey

As an early careers specialist, I see first hand the challenges and aspirations of young professionals navigating their exciting yet complex stage of life. Many find themselves chasing success without finding their true purpose and career fulfilment.

Pete offers a refreshing approach by providing inspiring insights and practical tools to help individuals align their lives with their values.

Readers will close this book with the blueprint for transforming aspirations into reality, offering a clear path to a more purposeful and satisfying life.

Amber Earl – early careers manager, Informa

Helps you think about who you are, how you show up and your impact on the world. This book is an easy read, and there's plenty of guidance for turning principles into practice. I also love that there's a chapter dedicated to embracing inclusion.

Catherine Garrod – author of *Conscious Inclusion* and founder of Compelling Culture

The
Better
Human
Blueprint

Self-development
strategies for personal
growth, success and
finding fulfilment

Pete Cooper

The Better Human Blueprint
ISBN 978-1-915483-69-0 (paperback)
ISBN 978-1-915483-70-6 (ebook)
ISBN 978-1-915483-71-3 (audiobook)

Published in 2024 by Right Book Press
Printed in the UK

© Pete Cooper 2024

The right of Pete Cooper to be identified as the author of this work has been asserted in accordance with the Copyright, Designs and Patents Act 1988.

A CIP record of this book is available from the British Library.

Contents

Finding fulfilment

Are you looking for fulfilment? If so, I've written this book for you. Fulfilment is deeply personal, and defining it is your journey. My role is to equip you with tools from evidence-based psychology, expert insights and real-life stories, and guide you towards your version of fulfilment.

I advocate for becoming a 'better human' – one committed to self-improvement and something greater than yourself. True fulfilment doesn't hinge on outcomes but on the pursuit itself. Embrace the journey, relish the moments and progress without falling into the trap of constant comparison. As Rugby World Cup winner Jonny Wilkinson eloquently shared on *The High Performance Podcast*, striving for 'better' rather than 'best' keeps our potential limitless (Humphrey & Hughes Sep 2020).

This book offers an invitation to continuous self-improvement, rather than presenting a final destination.

My personal journey

From an early age, I was driven more by the development of others in competitive tennis than by personal achievements. My decision to focus on coaching over competing was influenced by immediate benefits, including financial incentives. Yet it was also a profound indicator of my inherent passion for nurturing growth in others, a theme that has defined my career.

My fascination with psychology, a discipline that seeks

to understand human behaviour, began at around the same time. This interest propelled me to pursue a master's degree in occupational psychology, where I explored the essence of success and high performance. My curiosity didn't stop at academic study but extended to consuming a vast array of self-development resources, ranging from books and podcasts to TED talks and conferences.

Throughout my varied career, spanning the public, private and voluntary sectors, and roles from project management to consultancy, the constant theme has been working closely with people. My experiences have allowed me to apply psychological theories and models in practical settings, enhancing team performance, as well as individual and organisational growth through training, coaching, mentoring and leading cultural development programmes.

This constant engagement with new ideas, coupled with my critical approach to the 'so what?' of information, inspired me to write this book. It's not just about gathering knowledge but about understanding its practical implications. In a world overwhelmed by information and self-proclaimed experts, determining which resources are truly valuable can be daunting.

That's where this book comes in. It distils insights from industry experts into accessible advice with a strong emphasis on practical application. It's designed for anyone at the start of their career, those preparing for leadership roles, or individuals simply seeking to lead a more fulfilling life.

If you find yourself standing in a bookstore or browsing online, wondering where to start, consider this your gateway. Engage with the key topics that unveil the secrets to fulfilment, apply the techniques in the practical application sections, and delve deeper using the recommended resources that capture your interest.

Fulfilment strands

My diverse experiences in psychology and consultancy have not only enriched my understanding of human behaviour but crystallised my belief in a structured approach to fulfilment. Drawing on extensive research, I've distilled fulfilment into three essential elements: building meaningful foundations, aligning your actions with these foundations and forging meaningful connections. Just as a rope of three strands is far stronger, true fulfilment emerges when all of these elements seamlessly intertwine.

Each section of this book takes you through one of these three strands:

➔ **Meaningful foundations:** Explore how high self-awareness of your thoughts and feelings sets a direction for your life. Develop a clear understanding of what you stand for, where you want to go and how you can show up as your true self.
➔ **Meaningful alignment**: Learn to bridge the gap between your thoughts and actions and make better decisions.
➔ **Meaningful connections:** Delve into the dynamics of successful personal and professional relationships, effective leadership and how to contribute to a more inclusive society.

Fulfilment foes

As you strive for fulfilment, beware of three psychological pitfalls that I term 'fulfilment foes':

➔ **Arrival fallacy**: This is a pervasive misconception that achieving specific goals (such as a promotion, buying a house or getting married) will lead to lasting happiness. This belief can significantly undermine your foundations because it shifts your focus from enjoying the present to waiting for an idealised future.

➔ **Cognitive dissonance**: This occurs when there's a mismatch between what you believe and how you behave, creating unpleasant mental discomfort. For instance, if you value financial security but frequently engage in impulse buying, this conflict will lead to stress and unhappiness.

➔ **Empty relationships**: In the context of fulfilment, empty relationships refer to connections that lack depth, meaning or support, all of which are vital for psychological wellbeing. This foe highlights the importance of cultivating relationships that are not only fulfilling but also contribute positively to your emotional and mental health.

As you work through this book, each fulfilment foe will be addressed by the insights and exercises in the chapters, enabling you to avoid these pitfalls and take proactive steps towards finding fulfilment. Use these end-of-chapter exercises not just as tasks to complete but as opportunities to experiment and learn about yourself. I invite you to engage actively by applying what you learn in real-world scenarios and reflect on those experiences regularly.

Key themes

In addition to the key concepts specific to each topic in this book, there are overarching themes that recur throughout. Understanding these themes will not only enhance your understanding but better equip you to apply what you've learned. Below are some of the themes that form the core of this book.

➔ **Mental fitness:** Much like physical fitness helps our body to function optimally, mental fitness ensures our cognitive and emotional health is at its best. This theme advocates for treating wellbeing proactively, engaging in exercises to improve our fitness, rather than only considering our mental health when something's wrong and in need of restoration. Just as you may go to a gym to work on your physical fitness, many of the practical exercises in this book can be seen as opportunities to work on your mental fitness.

→ **Counselling versus self-development:** When considering personal growth, it's vital to distinguish between self-development and the therapeutic process. This distinction ensures that individuals seek appropriate support tailored to their specific needs, enhancing their overall wellbeing and the effectiveness of their efforts. Recognising when to opt for therapy instead of, or alongside, self-development is crucial. If past traumas or current mental health issues are affecting your daily life, self-development exercises are causing you stress or you're experiencing feelings of overwhelm, then I encourage you to consider professional counselling.

→ **Psychological safety**: This is the shared belief, held by team members, that it's OK to speak up, take risks and be creative without fear of humiliation or retribution. It's pivotal for innovation and teamwork in any setting (Edmondson 2018).

→ **Challenge network:** This consists of trusted individuals who provide honest feedback. This theme emphasises the importance of surrounding yourself with people who will challenge your ideas and push you to grow.

To fully benefit from these themes, and the ones contained in each chapter, I'd recommend approaching this book with an attitude of curiosity and openness. It's this attitude that's ever present among high achievers – the insatiable drive to learn, to grow, to be better, whether it's the successful Olympic swimming coach Mel Marshall, who advises us to 'go to sleep an expert and wake up a novice'; the New Zealand All Blacks, who continually evolve their game when at the top of their game; or prominent entrepreneurs such as Lewis Morgan, co-founder of Gymshark, who's constantly learning about new trends (Humphrey & Hughes Jul 2021; Kerr 2013; Humphrey & Hughes Apr 2022). This book will build on your drive for improvement, giving you the tools and techniques to propel you towards a fulfilling life and becoming a better human.

The shoulders of giants

Sir Isaac Newton famously remarked, 'If I have seen further than most, it is because I have been standing on the shoulders of giants.' This profound statement highlights the essence of intellectual advancement and personal growth, acknowledging that our achievements are often built upon the insights and discoveries of those who came before us. In this book, I draw heavily from the wisdom of several modern-day giants whose work has significantly influenced the fields of leadership, psychology and self-improvement and are a constant inspiration to me. Here's an introduction to some of these influential figures:

→ **Damian Hughes and Jake Humphrey**: Co-hosts of *The High Performance Podcast*, Hughes and Humphrey extract valuable life lessons from the experiences of high performers across various fields. Their discussions and books provide practical advice on achieving personal excellence and consistently maintaining high performance.

→ **Brené Brown**: A research professor known for her work on vulnerability, courage, empathy and shame – topics her bestselling books, podcasts and Netflix lecture (*The Call to Courage*) explore in detail.

→ **Simon Sinek**: Known for his inspiring talks on leadership and motivation as well as multiple books, Simon Sinek has introduced concepts such as the 'golden circle', which has revolutionised how organisations and leaders think about their purpose and strategy.

➔ **Steven Bartlett**: The youngest-ever investor on BBC One's *Dragons' Den* and a successful entrepreneur, Bartlett shares insights on entrepreneurship, leadership and overcoming obstacles through his podcast *Diary of a CEO* and his books.

➔ **Stephen Covey**: Author of *The 7 Habits of Highly Effective People*, Covey's work remains a cornerstone in personal and professional development literature, providing a framework for effectiveness based on character and principles.

➔ **Adam Grant**: An organisational psychologist who explores how human interactions can deeply influence workplace dynamics and personal success. Grant's books and podcasts provide actionable insights into creativity, motivation and the science of human behaviour.

By standing on the shoulders of these giants, this book aims to provide you with a comprehensive toolkit for personal and professional growth. In addition to my own experience and research, each chapter draws on their and others' ground-breaking ideas, allowing you to explore deeper insights and practical applications tailored to enhancing your journey towards fulfilment. Each chapter concludes with a 'Go deeper' section designed to facilitate further exploration and a deeper understanding of the topics covered.

As you progress through this book, remember to avoid the comparison trap. When it comes to finding fulfilment and becoming a better human, you're not competing against anyone else, just who you used to be.

Meaningful foundations

Chapter 1
Living your purpose

Live your purpose by understanding how your unique passions and skills can contribute to the needs of the world and by turning these into something you can be paid for.

Fulfilling careers

From a young age, the question 'What do you want to be when you grow up?' has echoed in my ears. It became clear early on that my dreams of lighting up the Premier League with my football skills or rocking out stadiums with my musical talent were far from reality. A strong realisation hit me during an engineering work experience placement that, while it served as an instructive and interesting detour, I was ill suited to the career I'd envisioned. As someone later reflected, considering my practical skills as an engineer, I'd make a great psychologist.

As with many of my peers, the pressure intensified as I selected academic subjects and progressed to choosing colleges, all without a clear vision of my future career. Thankfully, what I did know was that I wanted to work with people, a thought that steered me towards psychology. So far in my career, I've worked in jobs my teenage self had never heard of, an experience shared by many friends and family members. This insight, coupled with the rapid evolution of job roles, has led me to believe we've been asking the wrong question all along. Now, when I'm asked to speak about career management, I encourage people to see how this traditional question hinders rather than helps us in finding fulfilling careers.

The traditional Western perspective on careers adds undue pressure, leaving people wrestling with existential questions well into their professional lives. This outdated mindset keeps the elusive dream job forever out of reach, a pursuit that seems increasingly futile as the workplace undergoes significant transformation, with once-coveted career paths disappearing or evolving beyond recognition.

It's time for a paradigm shift in career development. We must move away from obsessing over specific job titles and towards aligning our motivations and skills with the ever-changing needs of society. The goal is not to find the perfect job but to advance our true purpose, adapting to the dynamic world of work with agility and openness. This approach not only promises greater personal fulfilment but also ensures our professional growth in a world where the only constant is change.

Fulfilling careers myth number one: follow the money

A common obstacle in the quest for fulfilling careers is the pervasive belief that financial success is a direct pathway to happiness. Encouraged by societal norms, this view positions the highest-paying jobs as the most desirable. However, this belief is fundamentally flawed, as it overlooks the concept of the hedonic treadmill, a finding that humans tend to return to a stable level of happiness or subjective wellbeing after experiencing increases in material wealth, quickly shifting their focus to the next financial milestone (Brickman & Campbell 1971). This phenomenon exemplifies the 'arrival fallacy', one of the fulfilment foes discussed in the introduction, illustrating the futility of seeking fulfilment solely through money or fame. It reveals the truth that there's no ultimate point of wealth, recognition or achievement that can provide lasting fulfilment if these are your sole pursuits. While money may resolve unhappiness, it won't give you lasting happiness.

The distinction between resolving unhappiness and cultivating happiness is supported by American psychologist Abraham Maslow's seminal theory of motivation, his hierarchy of needs (Maslow 1943). Maslow's pyramid begins with deficiency needs, fundamental requirements such as food and shelter, which need to be addressed to avoid discomfort. Once these basic needs are met, individuals can progress towards growth or psychological needs, pursuing self-improvement through relationships, respect and, ultimately, self-actualisation, where true fulfilment is found.

The film *Cast Away* (2000) featuring Tom Hanks as Chuck, who crash-lands on a deserted island, serves as an engaging illustration of Maslow's hierarchy in action. Chuck first satisfies his deficiency needs by fishing and drinking coconut water, then secures and later builds his own shelter. Having addressed these, he focuses on his growth needs, creating a companion called 'Wilson' from a volleyball to provide love and belonging, and attains self-esteem by mastering fire-making. Eventually, he achieves self-actualisation by building a boat to leave the island, symbolising his journey towards fulfilment.

When research, expert opinions and cultural narrative clichés all point in the same direction, it's wise to take note. The pursuit of wealth may offer short-term gains but will result in long-term dissatisfaction. Therefore, when evaluating your career choices and defining your purpose, it's essential to pay attention to the things you enjoy and find rewarding.

Fulfilling careers myth number two: follow your passion

The advice to 'follow your passion' is a staple in career guidance, resonating with appealing simplicity. However, when taken as standalone advice, it's fundamentally flawed. This notion rests on several assumptions: you have a single unchanging passion; you're already aware of it; and you're naturally skilled at it (Jachimowicz 2019; O'Keefe et al 2018). This advice can misleadingly suggest that if you simply follow your passion, your dream job will materialise effortlessly; whereas, in reality, your passions require dedication and can even be cultivated through hard work.

Many people have multiple passions that evolve over time, and these interests provide valuable insights into the types of careers you may find rewarding. Yet they're only a part of the bigger picture. To pursue a fulfilling life, you also need to identify your purpose. Simon Sinek refers to this as finding your 'why', a 'compelling higher purpose that inspires you and acts as the source of all you do' (Sinek 2011).

Your purpose doesn't need to be grandiose or filled with jargon to be meaningful. While society may press you to align your purpose with charitable or altruistic goals, and that's admirable if it resonates with you, it's not mandatory. What's vital is that your purpose is focused on something beyond yourself and personally significant.

A new approach to career management: finding your *ikigai*

The traditional Japanese philosophy of *ikigai* offers profound insights into the pursuit of a fulfilling career. Ikigai, which roughly translates as 'the happiness of always being busy', encapsulates the essence of finding joy and purpose in daily activities. It represents the driving force that gets you out of bed every day. Embracing your ikigai means living in alignment with what makes you feel genuinely fulfilled, combining what you love, what you're good at, what the world needs and what you can be paid for.

The power of living according to your ikigai is perhaps best exemplified by the residents of Okinawa, Japan. This island is renowned for having the highest proportion of centenarians in the world. Okinawans not only enjoy longer lives but also suffer from fewer chronic illnesses and have a below average rate of dementia. Research into regions with exceptionally high average lifespans, known as Blue Zones, highlights finding a purpose in life as a key ingredient for longevity. This goes hand in hand with other vital factors such as a healthy diet, regular exercise and strong social connections (García & Miralles 2017).

Incorporating the concept of ikigai into your career choices encourages you to look beyond the superficial allure of money or social status. It invites you to consider deeply what brings you joy, satisfaction and a sense of contribution to the broader community. By aligning your career with your ikigai, you not only enhance your own wellbeing but also contribute to a healthier, more fulfilled society.

The concept of ikigai is compelling precisely because it addresses multiple facets of life and career development. It not only emphasises the importance of pursuing what you love but also underscores the necessity of honing your skills through dedication and effort. But ikigai goes beyond these two aspects, suggesting that a fulfilling career requires alignment with societal needs and financial viability. The importance of balancing these two needs was reflected in a note handed to Bob Iger (2019), the CEO of Disney, by his former boss Dan Burke, which said: 'Avoid getting into the business of manufacturing trombone oil. You may become the greatest trombone oil manufacturer in the world, but in the end, the world only consumes a few quarts of trombone oil a year!' The principles of ikigai are echoed by those of entrepreneur Steven Bartlett (2021), who describes a dream job as one that's engaging, helpful to others and aligned with our talents. So, instead of pressuring yourself, or indeed your children, with the question of what you/they want to be when you/they grow up, you need to instead focus your energy on understanding your ikigai.

Although the Western interpretation of ikigai often focuses on career fulfilment, it's imperative to recognise that being purpose driven isn't confined to your professional life. Your ikigai could be unrelated to your career; it could revolve around building a loving family or contributing to your community. These are no less valid forms of purpose than those found in the professional realm. If you find yourself in a job that serves to finance such a purpose, I still encourage you to seek roles that align with your ikigai. Work consumes a sizeable portion of your life and aligning it with your ikigai can make that time more meaningful and rewarding. This is beautifully illustrated by the story of a janitor at NASA who, when asked about his role by President Kennedy, replied, 'I'm putting a man on the moon', capturing the profound impact a sense of purpose can bring to even the humblest occupations.

Infinite purpose

The idea of an infinite purpose may sound grandiose, but it's far from corporate jargon or a catchphrase. As often discussed by Simon Sinek, an infinite purpose is never truly fulfilled, but outlasts us and keeps us pushing for greater things. The notion of an infinite purpose stems from the philosophies of infinite and finite games first discussed by James Carse (1986). Unlike finite games, which have well-defined rules and clear winners and losers, infinite games, such as relationships, education, health, careers and life itself, have no finish line. While competitive elements exist in various aspects of life, including business and politics, exceptional leaders adopt an infinite mindset. They focus on advancing their organisations and teams rather than fixating on defeating their competitors. This is a focus that consistently delivers results, fostering higher levels of trust, cooperation and innovation (Sinek 2019).

The infinite mindset also underscores the importance of a purpose that you're 'for' rather than one you're 'against'. Aiming towards something not only sustains your motivation over the long term but better equips you to adapt to unexpected challenges, innovate more and attract more collaboration (Sinek 2019). A compelling illustration of this can be found in the New Zealand rugby team, one of the most successful sports teams ever. Instead of framing their purpose as becoming the world's number one team, a finite goal for a finite game, or defeating other teams, being against something, they articulate it as 'leaving the shirt in a better place' (Kerr 2013). This infinite perspective enables them to continually strive for excellence, rather than merely aiming for short-term victories.

Purpose-led decision making

A clear benefit of a well-defined purpose is its role as a guiding light while you navigate tough decisions, especially during complex situations where no clear-cut answers are available. When it comes to career moves, a concrete understanding of your purpose allows you to evaluate prospective organisations and determine if they're a good fit for you. While I'll delve deeper into effective decision-making strategies in Chapter 5, a straightforward approach is to ask whether the decision you're trying to make will advance your purpose. Below are some real-life instances, drawn from my own experiences, that illustrate how an understanding, or lack thereof, of your purpose can influence your decision making.

First, in my early twenties, I grappled with the choice between pursuing a master's degree in forensic psychology or one in occupational psychology. I was fascinated by both fields and had hands-on experience in each. After much debate, I opted for occupational psychology, swayed by its career prospects. In retrospect, I realise that I was subconsciously sifting through the facets of my ikigai without being explicitly aware of it. If I'd already identified my purpose back then, the decision-making process would've been considerably easier.

Second, when I was umpiring club field hockey, I had the opportunity to pursue doing so at a higher level. At around the same time, I was offered a position as the umpire development lead at my local club. The travel commitments of higher-level umpiring would prevent me from doing both roles to the best of my ability, meaning I felt I had to choose between them. Thanks to my keen awareness of my purpose, the decision was surprisingly straightforward. When questioned by a club player about choosing to stay local, I explained that contributing to the development of local umpires resonated more with me and was, for me, a more meaningful achievement. It was knowing my purpose that shielded me from external pressures and validated my choice, a decision I continue to find fulfilling.

By being purpose driven, you arm yourself with a powerful tool that not only streamlines your choices but also ensures they are deeply aligned with who you are and what you aspire to be.

Application
Turning principles into practice

Define what you love

The first step is to compile a list of what genuinely excites you. If you find this difficult, consider what makes you feel most alive, what you keep coming back to and what you consistently have energy for. True passions often don't need to be reignited, even if there are moments when they may seem challenging to pursue.

You could have a single passion or several. A useful method for identifying these is to reflect on your proudest accomplishments or personal highlights, both in your career and personal life.

Another strategy is to perform a time and motion study. Reflect on your activities over a specific period, paying attention to what you enjoyed and what you didn't, as well as what energised or drained you. Identifying patterns and commonalities will help you paint a clearer picture of your passions.

Questions to get you thinking:

- ✦ Are there moments when you become lost in an activity and time seems to stand still? What are you doing during those times?
- ✦ What kind of activities do you find rewarding?
- ✦ Given the choice, how do you prefer to spend your time?
- ✦ When do you feel most energised?
- ✦ What activities make you forget to eat or sleep?
- ✦ To what extent are you emotionally invested in your work?
- ✦ What do you enjoy learning about in your free time?
- ✦ What projects or tasks do you take on without being asked?
- ✦ What would you do even if you weren't getting paid for it?
- ✦ What types of activities make you feel most like yourself?

+ Are there recurring themes or subjects that consistently capture your interest?
+ What kind of problems do you enjoy solving?

What does the world need?

Having identified your passions, shift your focus towards understanding what the world needs. Don't just think about paid employment; think about the problems and opportunities facing the world today. This could be an overwhelming task, so try to narrow down your focus to the areas you feel passionate about. An alternative approach is to consult sources such as the organisation 80,000 Hours, a not-for-profit that offers insight into the world's most pressing issues.

Questions to get you thinking:

+ What causes or issues do you feel passionate about?
+ When do you feel you are making a difference?
+ Of your passions, which of them will still be around in 50 years?
+ What are the gaps in your community or workplace that you think should be filled?
+ What are some trends you foresee becoming more significant in the future?
+ What are the skills or knowledge areas where you think most people could benefit from improvement?
+ Are there problems or issues you believe are neglected or underestimated?
+ What sort of legacy do you want to leave?
+ In which areas do you think you could make the most impact?
+ What issues or concerns keep you up at night?

By dedicating time to answer these questions thoughtfully, you'll be well on your way to pinpointing your ikigai. This clarity will not only serve you in making life and career decisions but also enrich your understanding of what brings you true fulfilment.

What are you good at?

As well as self-reflection and the feedback of others, consider using well-established assessment methods such as the CliftonStrengths assessment by Gallup, or Strengthscope®. Remember that skill development is a lifelong journey and, with the right type of practice, you can become good at almost anything. Therefore, don't discard potential talents simply because they appear difficult at the outset.

One of the most revealing aspects to explore is what comes effortlessly to you but seems to be a struggle for others. I've engaged in numerous career development conversations where clients undervalue their own talents, dismissing them as common sense. Yet, these so-called obvious skills can be your unique contributions to the world. The capacity to do something that seems like second nature to you but is a hurdle for others is a telling sign of a strength.

Questions to get you thinking:

✦ What do people come to you for?
✦ When are you at your best?
✦ When are you at your worst?
✦ What do people compliment you on?
✦ What are you proud of?
✦ What do you notice that others don't?
✦ If you were replaced by someone just as capable, what would people miss?
✦ What tasks or projects have you completed that felt effortless?
✦ Is there a particular subject where you often find yourself teaching or guiding others?
✦ What have you accomplished that you initially thought you couldn't?
✦ What areas do you feel you've made the most progress in over the past year?

+ Are there skills or talents you possess that you feel are underutilised?
+ What aspects of your work are you most confident in?
+ What are some things that you've been good at since childhood?

What can you be paid for?

This question, particularly in a Western context, serves as a bridge between your purpose and your ikigai. A useful approach to tackling this question is to scour online job boards to gain insights into the skills and talents organisations are currently seeking. At this point, try not to fixate on whether you have the qualifications or experience to be eligible for the role. Instead, focus on which roles genuinely catch your interest, capturing details that resonate with you.

Questions to get you thinking:

+ Are there established jobs or career pathways in your current areas of interest?
+ Which career pathways have similar or overlapping skills to the one you're in currently?
+ What do people you know with similar interests do for a career?
+ Which jobs or career paths appeal to you?
+ If you have a hobby, is there a market or demand for the things you make or do?
+ Which skills or talents do you have that are in high demand?
+ What are some emerging fields or industries that might require your skills or interests?
+ Is there a skill or service you can offer that others are willing to pay a premium for?
+ Which skills or services have people offered to pay you for, even if you haven't accepted?
+ Which additional skills could you acquire to increase your earning potential?

Crafting your purpose statement

After compiling your four lists, the next step is to articulate your purpose. While crafting this statement may prove more challenging than anticipated, it's important not to be discouraged, even if the process spans several weeks. However, complexity is not a requirement. Your statement doesn't need to be full of words that leave people reaching for a dictionary. Consider it a living statement, open to reflection and refinement over time.

I've done just this with my own statement over time. My core purpose has remained constant, but my understanding and articulation of it has deepened through experiences and self-discovery. Central themes of self-development, fostering growth in others and innovative thinking have always been present. A pivotal question for me was 'If you were replaced by someone just as capable, what would people miss?' This reflection helped crystallise my unique contribution and is reflected in my current statement.

➔ **Initial statement:** 'To develop others, so we can achieve more than we ever thought possible.' This statement captured my passion for growth and development, aligning with my natural inclinations and professional path in learning and development.

➔ **Second statement:** 'To think differently and enable development, so together we can achieve more than we ever thought possible.' Progressing in my career, I embraced my drive for innovation and recognised my preference for dynamic, project-based roles over repetitive tasks.

➔ **Current statement:** 'To pursue better, in myself and others, so we can achieve more than we ever thought possible.' This reflects my realisation that continuous improvement is at the heart of my purpose, even when faced with roles that seemed ideal but lacked the scope for ongoing growth and change.

Your purpose statement will benefit from being short, simple, easily understood and focused on the positive impact you aim to create. It's less about the specific actions (what) and more about the overarching intent (why).

A simple template to guide you is: 'To (action) so (result/impact).'

Here are additional real examples to inspire you:

✦ To build relationships and work behind the scenes, so that the show can go on.
✦ To live life with integrity and empathy and be a positive force in the lives of others.
✦ To venture where nobody else is willing to go as well as provide a service that everyone needs.
✦ I want to make it so that every person in the world can afford to start their own business.

Revisit your four lists. Are there recurrent themes? Do you feel a strong emotional pull towards particular words or phrases? If so, these could be compelling elements to include in your purpose statement. If aligning the 'What can you be paid for?' aspect with the other three proves challenging, you may have unearthed your purpose but need to consider how it fits within a broader career context. For instance, if empowering others to find their voice is central to your purpose, there are employment opportunities that align with this, as well as other avenues such as employee support networks.

For additional guidance, you might consider Simon Sinek's 'Find Your WHY' paid resource or explore career support options through the Amazing If website, created by the authors of *Squiggly Careers*.

The aim is to align your life with your newly discovered purpose. Whether that involves skill building, further study or even a career shift, the objective is clear: don't just identify your purpose; live it.

Navigating career transitions: should I stay or go?

If you're at a crossroads in your career, pondering whether to remain in your current position or seek new opportunities, there are several key considerations to guide your decision-making process. First, assess if your desire to stay is driven primarily by the comfort and security the role offers. If comfort is your only reason for staying, it's time to embrace change.

To determine if your current role contributes to a fulfilling life, consider four critical criteria: is it rewarding, are you learning something new, are you earning enough and do you have work-life harmony? Ideally, your role will satisfy all these elements. While it's sometimes acceptable to stay in a position that meets three out of these four criteria, if you're only achieving two, it may be time to contemplate a change.

Steven Bartlett's book *Happy Sexy Millionaire* (2021) offers a valuable perspective on this dilemma. A particularly resonant question from his quitting framework is: 'Is the effort required to improve a situation worth it?' Often, we measure our ability to cope with workplace challenges by our resilience, questioning if we're tough enough to endure them. However, this mindset, sustained over time, can adversely affect our mental health. Reframing the question to consider the worth of effort needed for change can illuminate our circumstances in a new light.

I once left a job where the politics and environment were draining. Despite being fully capable of 'surviving' in that setting, I concluded that it simply wasn't worth the effort. This experience taught me the importance of evaluating not just whether I could endure, but whether enduring was valuable to my overall wellbeing and career trajectory.

Finally, if you do decide it's time to move on, ensure you're running towards a new role rather than simply escaping an old one.

Key takeaways

→ Traditional approaches to career development, centred on landing a 'dream job', are outdated and need rethinking.

→ While financial incentives can be motivating, their impact is often short lived.

→ 'Follow your passion' is an oversimplified and potentially misleading piece of career advice.

→ To achieve true fulfilment, you need to discover your ikigai, the intersection of what you love, are good at, can be paid for and what the world needs.

→ Rather than short-term goals, you will benefit from cultivating an 'infinite purpose', striving for something that outlives you.

Go deeper

→ *Ikigai*, Héctor García and Francesc Miralles

→ *Start with Why*, Simon Sinek

→ *Happy Sexy Millionaire*, Steven Bartlett

→ *The Squiggly Career*, Helen Tupper and Sarah Ellis

→ *The Infinite Game*, Simon Sinek

→ *Dare to Lead*, Brené Brown

→ *Drive*, Daniel H Pink

→ 'Navigating career turbulence', *WorkLife with Adam Grant*

Chapter 2
Emotional agility and resilience

Better understand yourself and others and equip yourself to face adversity.

Emotional intelligence

The capacity to understand and manage your emotions and to recognise and influence the emotions of others is a crucial factor in career success (Salovey & Mayer 1990). In fact, emotional intelligence is twice as significant as cognitive intelligence for workplace performance, accounting for nearly 90 per cent of success in leadership roles. While cognitive intelligence and education help you get a foot in the door, it's emotional intelligence that truly makes an impact. Beyond the professional realm, emotional intelligence enriches your personal life, fostering improved decision making and moral judgements, enhanced wellbeing and fulfilling relationships (Goleman 1998).

Two essential skills underpin emotional intelligence:

+ **emotional agility** – recognising, accepting and intentionally responding to our emotions (David 2017)
+ **resilience** – the strength and speed of our response to adversity (Sandberg & Grant 2019).

There are also some myths related to emotional intelligence that require debunking. Emotional intelligence is not about being nice. Sometimes, it involves confronting someone with an uncomfortable truth. Nor is it about wearing your heart on your sleeve; it's about managing your emotions and expressing them appropriately (Goleman 1998).

What are emotions?

What if almost everything you've been told about emotions was wrong? That's the premise of the theory of constructed emotion, introduced by Dr Lisa Feldman Barrett, a professor of psychology. Contrary to the traditional view of emotions as innate, uncontrollable reactions hardwired into our brains, recent scientific advancements suggest a different narrative. According to this theory, emotions are essentially predictions made by your brain, anticipating how you should feel in response to various experiences. These predictions originate from basic physiological sensations, such as calmness or agitation. However, these raw feelings await context to evolve into emotions. Without this context, they remain just summaries of what's going on inside your body. For example, a churning stomach might be experienced as hunger among appetising smells but anxiety in a medical setting (Feldman Barrett 2018).

It's important to emphasise that our cultural background plays a pivotal role in interpreting emotions. While you might believe you can read someone's emotions from their facial expression or body language, you are, in essence, making educated guesses based on your experiences and context – context that tells you that a smile means happiness, but it can also mean sadness or embarrassment, and there's such a thing as 'happy tears'. This highlights the importance of cultural sensitivity when trying to understand how other people are feeling.

A key implication of this theory is that you have more control over your emotions than is conventionally believed. Emotions serve as guides, not barriers, spotlighting your intrinsic values and encouraging you to make positive changes. This also means that while managing your emotional state may be challenging, it is possible. When facing nerve-wracking moments, rather than seeing your sensations as anxiety, consider them to be signals of readiness – your body gearing up for action. This is a reframe described as 'getting your butterflies to fly in formation' (Feldman Barrett 2018).

Understanding personal values

One of the clearest indicators of your personal values, or non-negotiables, is your emotional response to certain situations. These values represent what you consider most important in life, and strong reactions often signal that these values are being challenged. For example, I once witnessed someone discussing how their business excluded customers of certain nationalities. My intense emotional reaction and subsequent guilt for not speaking out highlighted inclusivity as one of my core values.

When you clearly understand your values, they can effectively guide your behaviour and decision making. While common values include fairness, family, kindness and generosity, it's important to invest time in defining your own values, as the same value can hold different meanings for different people. For instance, while one person may define success in terms of career achievements and tangible accomplishments, another may view success as a balanced life rich in personal satisfaction, family time and wellbeing.

It's also vital to refine your list of values so it doesn't become an exhaustive list of everything you care about, but rather focuses on topics that are truly central to you. In my experience, I've found identifying three core values is optimal. This not only helps others to understand you better but also forces you to prioritise what's most important. For instance, alongside inclusivity, my other core values are intentionality and authenticity.

Emotional agility

If emotions are our guides, emotional agility describes our ability to respond to these guides. Susan David, an award-winning Harvard Medical School psychologist, describes how becoming emotionally agile involves four pivotal stages (David 2017a):

+ **showing up** – embracing and labelling our emotions, viewing them as information rather than facts or directives
+ **stepping out** – gaining perspective, observing our emotions from a distance, acknowledging them as experiences rather than our identity
+ **walking our why** – making conscious choices aligned with our values
+ **moving on** – acting on those choices and fostering beneficial habits.

Emotional agility stands in contrast to two prevalent emotional coping strategies: bottling and brooding. While occasionally suppressing emotions (bottling) may be pragmatic, it's generally believed to be an unsustainable solution as it becomes damaging to our mental and physical health. Brooding might seem healthier since it recognises emotions, but it ties us to the past, amplifying anxiety. Emotional agility is distinct. It focuses on being present, curious and accepting of your emotions and thoughts, without assuming they're absolute truths (David 2017a).

One thing that gets in the way of emotional agility is categorising emotion as positive or negative. Masking discomfort with forced positivity prevents you from under-standing what these so-called 'negative' emotions are telling you, and what you can learn from them. Emotions such as anger and regret can spotlight areas you may want to ignore, places of weakness and areas for growth. For this reason, you must challenge the 'tyranny of positivity', not ignoring these difficult emotions, but understanding and responding to the message behind them (David 2017a,b).

To effectively navigate your emotions, it's pivotal to distinguish and label them accurately. The subtleties between emotions such as sadness, loneliness and boredom, while nuanced, are critical in determining the appropriate course of action for your wellbeing. This depth of insight, known as emotional granularity, requires a refined under-standing of your emotional spectrum. To cultivate this emotional granularity, you must be attuned to the physical expressions of your emotions, pay attention to the historical and situational factors influencing them and be aware of your default reactions (Brown 2021). Brené Brown's *Atlas of the Heart* (2021) offers an expansive guide through this landscape, exploring a wealth of emotions and the experiences or thoughts that lead to them.

While better understanding your emotions may seem like a soft and fluffy exercise, it offers significant rewards, as those adept at identifying their emotions can better navigate day-to-day life. Additionally, this skill enables you to decipher the underlying messages of your emotions, guiding you towards rewarding situations and away from potential pitfalls. Furthermore, individuals who struggle to articulate their emotions often express them solely through anger, sometimes escalating to physical aggression. Rather than being a healthy outlet, this anger often conceals other feelings, masking life changes that are required (David 2017a).

Cultivating resilience

Resilience embodies your capacity to recover from setbacks, learn from your experiences and keep the show on the road. It requires you to acknowledge suffering as an inevitable part of life without feeling singled out by fate. Instead of wallowing in 'why me?', resilience is about concentrating on aspects within your control, accepting those that aren't

(Sandberg & Grant 2019). Additionally, it involves adopting an optimistic mindset, characterised by a balanced recognition that while things might not be OK now, they will be in the future.

Central to your response should be avoiding the 'three Ps' that work against emotional resilience: personalisation, pervasiveness and permanence (Seligman 2006). Personalisation is the tendency to think you are the problem rather than recognising the impact of other factors. For instance, author and technology executive Sheryl Sandberg describes how she blamed herself following her husband's death, despite being advised there was nothing she could have done. In her book *Option B* (2019), she also shares that it wasn't until she was convinced to stop blaming herself, stop apologising to those around her and realise factors outside her control were to blame that she was able to start moving forward (Sandberg & Grant 2019).

Pervasiveness refers to your inclination to let a setback bleed into every part of your life, a mindset that can be crippling. No matter how severe, adversity rarely overwhelms every aspect of your life and often, little by little, normality can be restored by focusing on those unaffected areas. Resilient individuals find comfort and refuge in these spaces, whether through activities such as music, art, sport or exercise, immersing themselves in these pursuits to the extent that other concerns momentarily fade away. It's essential, amid adversity, not to succumb to pervasiveness, which can discourage you from engaging with your passions and instil a sense of guilt for relishing the untouched joys that remain.

Permanence, which is the belief that a difficult situation will last forever, can be the most challenging 'P' to counteract. Unsurprisingly, those adept at seeing setbacks as temporary demonstrate greater resilience, adapting more readily to change.

Research into 'affective forecasting', predicting how we

will feel in the future, demonstrates people's tendency to misjudge their future emotions, often overestimating the intensity and duration of their distress (Celestine 2018). To combat this, we can all benefit from being intentional about the language we use, substituting absolutes such as 'always' and 'never' with temporary descriptors such as 'sometimes' and 'lately'. This linguistic shift can help us perceive adversity as a temporary obstacle rather than an endless plight, instilling the hopeful reminder that 'this too shall pass'.

Lucy Hone, a resilience expert who faced profound loss, recommends a practical approach to resilience: regularly assessing whether your actions help or harm you. Adopting this as her coping mechanism following her daughter's tragic accident, applying it in such decisions as choosing not to attend the driver's trial, underscores that resilience is deeply personal and varied in its expression. Embracing resilience means allowing yourself the space to discern what aids your recovery from adversity. It empowers you to make decisions that protect your mental health, practise self-compassion and stay firm in response to social pressure and the demands of others.

Application
Turning principles into practice

Mastering the basics

Breathe and anchor: Understanding the gap between the onset of emotions and your response is vital. It gives you the chance to widen this gap and choose responses that reflect your values. When you feel tense, focus on your breathing. Counting breaths, for instance, can help restore calmness.

You can also take inspiration from techniques such as the New Zealand All Blacks' 'anchoring' (Kerr 2013). They prepare for high-pressure moments by practising a physical action, such as scrunching toes or clenching a fist in a calm state, thereby linking the two. Then, in high-pressure situations, they repeat this action, triggering the calm state they have associated with it.

Think about a physical action you can use as your anchor. It's best if it's something simple you can do anywhere, anytime. With practice, this anchor can become a powerful tool to swiftly bring you back to a state of calm, even in the middle of emotional turmoil.

Take a break: Never underestimate the power of a brief time out. If you find yourself in a tense situation and the above techniques aren't quite cutting it, it's OK to step away. Offer a neutral reason, such as grabbing a drink or going to the bathroom, and use this time to process your emotions and return with a clearer head.

Emotional hygiene: Your physical habits significantly affect your emotional responses. Sleep, exercise, caffeine consumption and diet play critical roles in how you handle emotions. View self-care as essential, not optional – especially if you're often in a support role for others.

Remember that you can't pour from an empty cup. Regularly practising gratitude can transform your perspective, reducing stress and increasing overall happiness. It's more than just a feel-good habit; it's a proven method for improving emotional wellbeing.

Identifying your values

Discovering your core values is a transformative process that can clarify your decision making and improve your relationships. Here's a three-stage process to help you identify your values:

➜ **Step 1**: **List what's important.** Begin by listing the things in life you consider important. This could be anything from concepts such as freedom and security to more tangible elements such as family time or career success.

➜ **Step 2: Select your top three values.** From your list, choose the top three values that resonate the most with you. These values need to reflect the principles you consider most critical to how you live and work.

➜ **Step 3: Define your values in your own words.** Articulate what each chosen value means to you personally. This step ensures your values are tailored to your life and not just abstract concepts.

For example, my top three values are:

✦ **Intentionality**: I choose how I respond in every situation.
✦ **Authenticity**: I show up as my true self, acting in accordance with my purpose and beliefs.
✦ **Inclusivity**: I believe everyone deserves equal opportunities and strive for equity in all I do.

Reflective questions to further explore your values

To delve deeper into what shapes your beliefs and behaviours, consider these questions:

+ What do you believe in?
+ What would you fight for?
+ What makes you angry or upset?
+ When have you felt the proudest?
+ What situations have made you uncomfortable?
+ What do people value you for?
+ How would others describe you?
+ What inspires you?
+ What do you admire in others?
+ What do you want to be remembered for?
+ What do you find yourself discussing the most?
+ What are your 'non-negotiables'?
+ When do you feel most yourself?

These questions can help you identify patterns and themes that align with your core values. You may find useful insights in your answers from Chapter 1. For those seeking additional inspiration, resources such as the Dare to Lead hub (brenebrown.com/hubs/dare-to-lead) offer an extensive list of values for your consideration.

Once you've identified your values, share them with others. Don't assume that people know what drives you or that you share the same values. I've found sharing values is one of the fastest ways to connect with others on a meaningful level. It can lead to profound moments of connection, including tears, laughter and eye-opening revelations.

Developing emotional agility

Gain deeper insights into your emotional patterns through resources such as Susan David's Emotional Agility Insight report at susandavid.com/quiz. You can also find resources on the site such as: Emotional Granularity Checklists, Emotional Granularity Umbrellas and 5 Ways to Walk Your Why. Brené Brown's Atlas Hub (brenebrown.com/hubs/atlas-hub) is also an excellent resource for understanding and expanding your emotional vocabulary.

Journaling for emotional clarity

The method below, known as Pennebaker's writing method (2004), can offer profound insights into your emotional world:

+ Commit to writing for 15–20 minutes each day for four days.
+ Focus on your emotional experiences from the past week or month.
+ Let your thoughts flow without worrying about grammar or spelling. Remember, this is a personal exercise for your eyes only.

After completing these four days, you'll have the flexibility to adjust this practice to suit your needs. Whether you continue journaling daily, or opt for a less frequent schedule, the key is to establish a routine that feels right for you. There's compelling research to suggest that regularly showing up to write, or even speak into a voice recorder, about your emotions can have tremendous benefits for your emotional and physical health. This isn't just about writing; it's about engaging with your emotions in a consistent and mindful way, creating a space for self-reflection and growth.

Cultivating resilience

To cultivate resilience, you need to challenge the three Ps: personalisation, pervasiveness and permanence. Below is an example of how you can reframe a scenario:

+ **Situation**: Unsuccessful job interview.
+ **Personal**: 'I'm a failure.'
+ **Permanent**: 'I'll never find a job.'
+ **Pervasive**: 'Everything in my life is going wrong.'

Now, reframe it.

+ **Impersonal**: 'Another candidate had more experience.'
+ **Temporary**: 'The right job for me is out there.'
+ **Specific**: 'This setback is limited to my professional life. I have fulfilling relationships, a vibrant social life and hobbies that bring me joy.'

Again, language is at the heart of cultivating resilience so really pay attention to how you're articulating your experiences, both to others and in your own self-talk. Make sure you're adopting language that's impersonal, temporary and specific.

Key takeaways

➜ Emotions aren't hardwired, uncontrollable reactions in the brain; they're spotlights providing you with useful information.

➜ Emotions are something you feel, not something you are, and you need to show up and pay attention to what you're experiencing.

➜ You need to take care of your emotional hygiene, viewing self-care as essential, not optional.

➜ You need to develop your emotional granularity, building up your emotional glossary, to truly understand how you're feeling.

➜ You can cultivate resilience by resisting the temptation to experience adversity as permanent, pervasive and personal.

Go deeper

➜ *How Emotions are Made*, Lisa Feldman Barrett

➜ *Emotional Agility*, Susan David

➜ *Atlas of the Heart*, Brené Brown

➜ *Option B*, Sheryl Sandberg and Adam Grant

➜ *Working with Emotional Intelligence*, Daniel Goleman

➜ *Inside Out*, Pixar

➜ Pippa Grange, *The High Performance Podcast*

➜ Owen O'Kane, *The High Performance Podcast*

➜ Mo Gawdat, *The High Performance Podcast*

Chapter 3

Vulnerability and authenticity

Root yourself in the knowledge that you are enough and practise vulnerability by being courageous, respecting boundaries and embracing uncertainty and emotional exposure.

What is vulnerability?

'It is not the critic who counts; not the man who points out how the strong man stumbles, or where the doer of deeds could have done them better. The credit belongs to the man who is actually in the arena, whose face is marred by dust and sweat and blood; who strives valiantly; who errs, who comes short again and again, because there is no effort without error and shortcoming; but who does actually strive to do the deeds; who knows great enthusiasms, the great devotions; who spends himself in a worthy cause; who at the best knows in the end the triumph of high achievement, and who at the worst, if he fails, at least fails while daring greatly, so that his place shall never be with those cold and timid souls who neither know victory nor defeat.'

The 'man in the arena' passage, an extract from a speech given by Theodore Roosevelt (1910), former president of the United States, serves as a cornerstone for Brené Brown, the world's leading expert on vulnerability. Brown often cites this passage to encapsulate the essence of vulnerability, calling it the 'call to courage'. She asserts that practising vulnerability is crucial as it fosters love, belonging, courage, joy,

41

connection, empathy and meaningful human experience. Moreover, it has significant advantages at the group level, including enhancing creativity, psychological safety and performance (Brown 2015a, 2018; Edmondson 2018).

What exactly is vulnerability? According to Brown (2018), it's an emotion tied to uncertainty, risk and emotional exposure. In essence, vulnerability isn't about winning or losing; it's about courageously facing unpredictable outcomes. Vulnerability also challenges the widespread cultural narrative of rugged individualism, which idolises self-reliance and stigmatises asking for help as a sign of weakness. Contrary to this, true vulnerability isn't a sign of weakness; it's a mark of strength. It's the courage to show up, ask for help and embrace discomfort, knowing the risks involved. Vulnerability is also something you can practise, recognising that to do so will involve failing and having the courage to pick yourself up again (Brown 2015b).

Practising vulnerability can manifest in numerous ways, depending on the context and the people involved. Common examples include:

+ **expressing love** – saying 'I love you' first, without knowing it will be said back
+ **sharing feelings** – discussing fears, insecurities, hopes and dreams with friends or a partner
+ **apologising** – admitting you were wrong and saying sorry, especially when it's difficult
+ **giving and getting feedback** – actively asking for advice and giving constructive feedback
+ **saying 'I don't know'** – being the first person to admit this in a meeting
+ **innovation** – proposing a new idea or project, knowing it might fail or be rejected
+ **pushing yourself** – whether a new task, skill or activity; doing something that scares you. This can be as simple as going on a new rollercoaster ride.

Vulnerability and self-worth

One of the most damaging lies you can tell yourself is that you're not enough. You may misguidedly gauge your self-worth through external factors such as appearance, job title, social media following, relationship status and the opinions of others. However, you need to grasp the fundamental truth that you're valuable, lovable and essential to this life. There's no minimum criterion for self-worth; you define it. The liberating truth? You're already enough.

Your self-worth is the foundation for practising vulnerability. It serves as an anchoring point, much like how infants use their parents as safe bases when exploring the world. Because true belonging requires the courage to present your authentic self, you'll only experience it when you truly accept who you are. As you practise vulnerability, stepping outside your comfort zone and encountering inevitable failures, maintaining a keen sense of self-worth safeguards you from internalising failure as an identity rather than as an experience. In moments like these, it would serve you well to extend yourself the same grace you offer others, viewing vulnerability as an act of courage and openness rather than as a sign of weakness. You need to remember that failure is something you do, not someone you are. Failure is an action, not an identity.

Vulnerability and shame

The biggest barrier to practising vulnerability is shame, an intensely painful feeling or belief that you're flawed, unlovable, unworthy of connection and don't belong. Shame is distinct from guilt; the focus is on the self rather than behaviour. For example, 'I am stupid' rather than 'I did something stupid'. Shame isn't a driver of positive change or behaviour. It embodies the fear that if someone uncovers something specific about you, they will no longer want to know you. It's the 'I am not enough' sentiment everyone encounters at various points in their lives.

To be truly vulnerable, you must confront and move past shame. Shame is the direct opposite of courage and keeps you on the outside, judging others and spotlighting their shortcomings, often in the areas in which you feel most vulnerable yourself (Brown 2015a).

While it's not possible to entirely avoid or resist shame, developing shame resilience is achievable, either through working with those close to you or with a trained counsellor/therapist. Shame resilience is the practice of remaining authentic when you experience shame, navigating the experience with courage, adhering to your values and suffering disappointment without diminishing your self-worth. Ultimately, shame resilience is about extending to yourself the compassion and love you offer those you care about (Brown 2018).

As practising vulnerability involves pushing past shame and embracing uncertainty, risk and emotional exposure, it's arguably the most courageous thing you can ever do. In fact, Brown argues that no act of courage is possible without vulnerability. However, the courage required here is different to the Hollywood bravery often idolised in the Western world. The courage needed to practise vulnerability is the courage to do the right thing over the easy thing, to ask for help and allow ourselves to be seen, truly and deeply seen (Brown 2015a). The courage needed for vulnerability is the courage to get up one more time than you fall.

Vulnerability in the workplace

The phrase 'bring your whole self to work' has become as ubiquitous in company cultures as 'thinking outside the box' or 'blue sky thinking'. But beyond its clichéd status, what does it truly mean to bring your whole self to work, and is it genuinely advisable?

In my experience working with teams and organisations committed to the principle of authenticity, I've witnessed environments where individuals can truly be themselves, aligning their actions with personal values and principles. This authenticity isn't merely beneficial; it's essential for wellbeing, personal integrity and fulfilment. Moreover, the failure to live authentically introduces cognitive dissonance, the second fulfilment foe. This unsettling discomfort arises when your actions don't align with your beliefs, not only eroding your sense of integrity but also obstructing your path to genuine fulfilment.

Vulnerability and authenticity share a tight-knit relationship. In essence, all acts of vulnerability demand authenticity, but not every authentic act requires vulnerability. Authenticity fundamentally means living according to your values, making decisions that are in line with these and not compromising on these to fit in. It means standing up for what you believe in, even in difficult circumstances, whatever the consequences.

Early in my career, while working for a recruitment company, I suffered a significant amount of cognitive dissonance. My breaking point came when I was asked to register as a candidate with a competitor to gather intelligence, a task that made me feel incredibly uncomfortable. I refused, and this experience, coupled with feedback that 'I cared too much about people to be good at the job', was a clear indication my 'true self' wasn't welcome there. This experience underscored the importance of seeking organisations aligned with my values, teaching me a valuable lesson about the necessity of authenticity in the workplace.

However, embracing your 'whole self' at work is more nuanced, as this involves vulnerability. In this context, it's vital to remember vulnerability isn't about airing your deepest secrets indiscriminately or oversharing in a cathartic purge. Authentic vulnerability involves sharing your experiences and emotions with those who've earned your trust (Brown 2015a). Authentic vulnerability respects boundaries. Therefore, if you practise true vulnerability, it's not only appropriate but also beneficial to bring your whole self to work.

A note of caution: every time you practise vulnerability, it involves risk, and this is especially pertinent in workplaces lacking in psychological safety. In such settings, the potential rewards of vulnerability may not outweigh the risks. However, if you find yourself in such a workplace, it's worth considering a change for one that values psychological safety and will better enable you to find fulfilment.

Knowing what to share

As authentic vulnerability respects boundaries, you need a way of deciding what's appropriate to share. The key to this lies in understanding your motivations for being vulnerable. The primary goal must be to deepen a relationship with someone, or a group of people, who have earned your trust. Vulnerability should never be used as a shortcut to intimacy or as a test for the strength of a relationship. Nor should it be employed to seek emotional relief from those who haven't yet earned that level of intimacy with you. At its core, vulnerability is about connecting with the right person, at the right time, about the right thing (Brown 2010).

A story from a friend of mine effectively illustrates the importance of establishing boundaries. After losing a child, they found themselves struggling to answer the question 'How many children do you have?', especially when meeting new people. Sharing the loss often resulted in an uncomfortable silence, yet omitting that child felt like betraying their memory. Considering this issue through a lens of whether the person had earned the right to hear their story shifted the focus. It enabled them to evaluate whether there was a sufficient emotional connection to warrant sharing such a deeply personal aspect of their life. It provided a different angle to consider, one that's more about readiness and relationship than mere disclosure.

Don't be an authentic arsehole

However, authenticity isn't a free pass to behave recklessly, ignoring social cues or the feelings of others. If someone defends rudeness with claims of 'I'm just being honest' or 'I'm just being myself', they're missing the point. They aren't being compassionate or considerate; they're just being themselves at the expense of others. Authenticity without empathy is selfish, and in the extreme, narcissistic. Wharton professor Adam Grant nails this sentiment, advising, 'Be yourself, unless yourself is an arsehole.' (Grant Apr 2020)

Let's debunk a myth: authenticity isn't an excuse for poor preparation. I die a little inside when I hear someone say 'I haven't prepared, so you're getting the real me' before a presentation. This is an abuse of 'authenticity' and shows a complete disregard for those on the receiving end of whatever ill-thought-out rubbish they're about to receive.

Charles Green's 'trust equation' succinctly captures this idea: trust equals credibility plus reliability plus intimacy, all divided by self-interest. Authenticity fosters trust only when it's complemented by competence and concern for others (Grant Apr 2020; Trusted Advisors).

The armour of vulnerability

There are many shields that people employ to sidestep true vulnerability, shields Brown refers to as 'suits of armour' – oversharing being just one. While each suit is different, they're all designed to keep you safe, in control, with everyone at a safe distance. While children have no problems being innocent, open and honest, often to the embarrassment of their parents, as teenagers we become hypersensitive to the opinions of others and it's at this point we learn to put on our armour, which inadvertently becomes a barrier to the authentic belonging we seek. As adults, we therefore must learn to take off the armour and practise vulnerability as we strive for connection.

Brown identifies several forms of armour that centre on dampening emotional experience. These include 'vulnerability numbing', which is used to blunt negative emotions; 'foreboding joy', the inability to fully appreciate beautiful moments due to fear of impending doom; and 'controlling situations', which can manifest as either micromanagement or emotional detachment. Unfortunately, it's not possible to minimise the negative side of emotions without limiting the positive, and therefore while this armour is designed to protect you, it usually ends up as a barrier to experiencing the full spectrum of human emotions, especially joy. When you try to shut out darkness, you also shut out the light (Brown 2015a).

The perils of perfectionism

Perfectionism stands out as both the most prevalent and potentially harmful suit of armour. While it masquerades as a quest for excellence, it's rooted in a fear of criticism and failure. The perfectionist's rationale? 'If I'm perfect, I'll earn love and acceptance.' However, as perfection is impossible, this mindset often proves self-destructive, spiralling into shame and self-blame when the inevitable failures occur, especially when a failure results in a redoubling of efforts to be 'more perfect'. Perfectionism also kills innovation as it's difficult for perfectionists to rip up the rule book, take risks and try new things, especially when there's a good chance that it's not going to work every time.

While perfectionism has been linked to academic achievements, there's no such link with workplace performance. The reason for this is that academic success often has clear, 'correct' answers, whereas in the workplace, performance becomes more subjective and influenced by external factors (Harari et al 2018). Therefore, while perfectionism may appear to have some benefit in early life, it's important to remember it's not the key to success later on. In fact, it's far more likely to lead to burnout, anxiety, depression, addiction and other negative health factors (Brown 2015b).

There's a clear and important distinction between perfectionism and having a growth mindset (first defined by Carol Dweck), which is beneficial. An individual with a growth mindset seeks to improve, striving for excellence, whereas a perfectionist is concerned with avoiding criticism and managing the perception of others. This distinction surfaces most clearly when the individual experiences failure. When a growth-minded individual fails, they recognise it's their technique that's flawed and will focus on improving it. When a perfectionist fails, they're likely to internalise the failure, believing they themselves are flawed. This also explains why receiving criticism can be an especially painful experience for perfectionists (Grant May 2022). Perfectionists are also more likely to only attempt things that are either easy or borderline impossible, known as operating with a mindset of needing to avoid failure, as opposed to needing to achieve success (Atkinson & Feather 1974). This mindset can result in self-handicapping since they won't even attempt some things as they don't want to find out they aren't capable and therefore it's easier to not even try.

One of the ways of determining whether you're operating from a growth or perfectionist mindset is to consider where your focus is. Growth-minded self-improvement is, as the name suggests, self-focused, asking how you can improve; whereas perfectionism is other-focused, asking what they'll think (Grant Apr 2020). This self-versus-other focus also highlights an incredibly dangerous trap it's amazingly easy to fall into: the comparison trap. There's nothing to be gained from comparing yourself to others and doing so is guaranteed to rob you of joy. Life is an infinite game, and you're not competing with anyone else; remember the only person you ever need to compete with is the person you were yesterday.

Before considering how to overcome perfectionism in

the application section below, it's important to remember two core truths. First, your self-worth isn't determined by achievements or external validation; you are enough, simply by virtue of being you. Second, we could all benefit from adopting Adam Grant's suggested definition of success as being less about achieving perfection and more about overcoming struggles (Grant May 2022).

Application
Turning principles into practice

Understand your self-worth

One way of understanding your level of self-worth, and where you draw this from, is to complete the Contingencies of Self-Worth Scale. This scale evaluates your self-worth across seven different domains: family support, competition, appearance, God's love, academic competence, virtue and approval from others (Crocker et al 2003).

An alternative approach is to consider this scenario: envision that all your possessions, career, money, relation-ships, friendships and accomplishments were suddenly stripped away. Reflect on this question: if all I were left with was myself, what valuable aspects would remain?

Take your time and answer this honestly, as your response serves as the measure of your self-worth.

To deepen your understanding, consider answering these questions:

+ Who am I?
+ What key moments in life define who I am today?
+ What is my purpose?
+ What am I good at?
+ What is my contribution to my relationships/community/work?
+ How do I define success, and why do I define it that way?
+ What do I admire most in others, and do I see any of those qualities in myself?
+ How would the people who know me best describe me?

Practise self-compassion

Building genuine self-worth requires a thorough and honest self-assessment, embracing both your strengths and weaknesses, warts and all. Acknowledging that nobody

The Better Human Blueprint

is perfect allows you to forgive your past mistakes, accept your current self and move forward. Resources such as the Self-Compassion Research lab, led by Dr Kristin Neff, a pioneer in the study of self-compassion, offer various exercises and information on how to practise self-compassion. You can find these tools at self-compassion.org and exercises such as 'writing a letter to yourself' and 'taking care of the care giver' are highly recommended. If you've experienced trauma or struggle with deep-rooted shame, consider seeking professional counselling while working through these exercises.

An effective strategy to challenge your inner critic is to employ daily affirmations. Repeating phrases such as 'I am enough just as I am' or 'I am deserving of love and respect' can significantly reinforce your self-worth. You'll also benefit from working through the exercise on challenging limiting beliefs exercise in Chapter 4.

Accepting compliments can be a challenge. If this is the case for you, work on acknowledging them with a thank you rather than dismissing them out of hand. Make it a practice to silently repeat each compliment you receive. Alternatively, write it down and place it in a 'compliment jar': a useful resource for moments when you need a boost. A list of affirmations written by a youth group I once worked with provided me with a significant boost during a tough time years later.

Your environment significantly influences your sense of self-worth. Immerse yourself in activities and communities that align with your interests and values and consider how the people around you affect you. Look to spend time with people who make you feel good about yourself and stop spending, or at least minimise, the time you spend with people who negatively impact you.

Danielle Koepke, writer and founder of the Internal Acceptance Movement, encapsulates this thought: 'You don't ever have to feel guilty about removing toxic people from your life. It doesn't matter whether someone is a relative, romantic interest, employer, childhood friend, or a new acquaintance. You don't have to make room for people who cause you pain or make you feel small. It's one thing if a person owns up to their behaviour and makes an effort to change. But if a person disregards your feelings, ignores your boundaries, and continues to treat you in a harmful way, they need to go.'

As you develop your own self-worth, remember the power of uplifting others. Compliment your friends, family and colleagues on their qualities or achievements. Acts of kindness not only boost your own self-worth but also create a positive cycle of mutual respect and admiration.

Cultivating shame resilience

In order to cultivate shame resilience, it's imperative to first identify when you're in the grips of shame. Understand the physiological and behavioural symptoms and pinpoint what triggers them. Physiologically, you may experience time slowing down, blushing, sweating and an elevated heart rate, as well as broken speech or thoughts, even the dreaded 'going blank' (Traumatic Stress Institute 2007). On the behavioural front, you may exhibit patterns that fit into one of three 'strategies of disconnection': moving away, withdrawing or silencing yourself; moving towards, people pleasing; or moving against, becoming aggressive or employing shame as a weapon (Hartling et al 2000).

While these strategies offer a momentary escape, they perpetuate disconnection and undermine the very sense of belonging you seek. Therefore, it's essential to interrupt these behaviours. Reflect on these questions, perhaps even discussing them with those close to you:

✦ Who do I become when I experience shame?
✦ What are my most common triggers for experiencing shame?

53

+ How does shame manifest in my physical body? Are there sensations I can recognise as signals?
+ Can I identify a recent situation where shame led me to act in a way that didn't serve me or align with my values?
+ What coping mechanisms have I developed to deal with shame, and are they healthy or destructive?
+ What strategy for disconnection am I most likely to employ?
+ How does my shame affect those around me, including family, friends and colleagues?
+ How has my relationship with shame evolved over the years, and what life events have contributed to this?

The next step in building shame resilience requires another person's involvement. This might be a trusted friend, partner or professional counsellor. Although you can gain some insights by doing this exercise on your own, the value multiplies when shared.

→ **Practise critical awareness:** While engulfed in shame, our thoughts become self-centred. It's vital to challenge the thoughts and expectations fuelling your shame. Are they reasonable? Attainable? Are they aligned with your desires or merely what you assume others expect from you?

→ **Reach out and speak shame:** Shame feeds on secrecy and silence. By sharing your story, your experience and your current emotional state, you can weaken shame's grip and break the silence. Make sure you reach out to your challenge network for this conversation. It may even be helpful to keep a list of these key individuals for times when you need them.

As you share your thoughts with others, be alert to the gaslighting language of shame: phrases that minimise or belittle your experiences, such as 'you're too sensitive' or 'you're too defensive'. If you encounter such dismissiveness, re-evaluate that person's place in your network.

Practising vulnerability

This isn't about following complicated models or instruction manuals; it's a simple call to courage. The challenge comes in learning how to shed the various kinds of armour that prevent us from embracing vulnerability.

Armour 1: Minimising human experience

This set of protective behaviours – numbing, foreboding joy and controlling – arises from a reluctance to embrace the full range of human emotions. The antidote is simple: lean in and practise embracing life. Be present, pay attention and move forward. Work on acknowledging and appreciating the good moments instead of retreating when you feel vulnerable. Practise gratitude as a response to the churn of vulnerability, and you'll likely find your emotions shifting towards the positive (Brown 2015a).

Ask yourself the following questions:

✦ In which specific situations do I find myself numbing or foreboding joy?
✦ Can I recall moments when I opted for control rather than embracing the experience?
✦ How can I practise daily gratitude in my life to counteract these tendencies?

Armour 2: Oversharing

The key question with oversharing is 'How will I know when it's appropriate to share something with someone?' Reflect on your intentions before you share and evaluate whether you're being driven by any strong emotions that could lead to regret. The goal of sharing needs to be to drive connection, not to unload your issues on someone else.

Ask yourself the following questions:

✦ Has this person earned the right to hear my story?
✦ What have the outcomes been when I've overshared in the past?

+ Do I tend to overshare more with certain people or in certain situations?
+ What are my motives?

Armour 3: Perfectionism

Here are four techniques to help you manage perfectionism (Grant May 2022).

→ **Acknowledge excellence, not perfection:** Aim high, but don't let perfection get in the way of good enough. Define what 'good enough' means for you or your stakeholders at the outset.
→ **Measure progress, not comparison:** Gauge your performance based on your own previous efforts rather than comparing yourself to others.
→ **Cultivate a challenge network:** Just as you need trusted individuals to combat shame, you need them to fight perfectionism. Seek feedback from those you trust and listen to their constructive criticism along with their praise.
→ **Narrow your focus:** Overload of feedback can be distracting and demoralising. Identify a few key areas, or potentially just one thing, for improvement at a time.

Ask yourself the following questions:

+ What are the projects or areas of my life where perfectionism is most evident?
+ How does my desire for perfection impact those around me?
+ Can I think of a situation where I wasted time working on something that was already good enough?
+ Who's in my challenge network for feedback?

You can also explore the topic of vulnerability further at brenebrown.com/hubs as well as in the resources section on the same website.

Key takeaways

➜ You're already enough, just as you are.
➜ Vulnerability is the birthplace of belonging, courage and authenticity, and is not weakness.
➜ Practising vulnerability requires being courageous, developing shame resilience and embracing uncertainty and emotional exposure.
➜ Being vulnerable requires setting boundaries and must only be done to drive connection.
➜ Don't let perfection get in the way of good enough.

Go deeper

➜ *Daring Greatly*, Brené Brown
➜ Mel Robbins, *The High Performance Podcast*
➜ 'Authenticity is a double-edged sword', *WorkLife with Adam Grant*
➜ 'Breaking up with perfectionism', *WorkLife with Adam Grant*
➜ Hector Bellerin, *The High Performance Podcast*
➜ 'Meet yourself: a user's guide to building self-esteem', Niko Everett, TedxYouth@BommerCanyon

Meaningful
alignment

Chapter 4
Align your actions

Achieve fulfilment by choosing how you respond in every situation and making better decisions.

Self-awareness and metacognition

Back in 1995, McArthur Wheeler shamelessly robbed a bank in broad daylight. Despite not bothering with a face mask, he was shocked when he was arrested, as he believed that slathering his face in lemon juice would make him invisible to security cameras. Unsurprisingly, he was wrong. This is a textbook example of what psychologists call the Dunning–Kruger effect (Dunning 2011), when people who are bad at something are unaware of their incompetence, often wrongly believing themselves to be experts.

Reflecting on McArthur Wheeler's misguided confidence and the broader implications of the Dunning–Kruger effect, we see the critical role self-awareness plays in recognising our own limitations and capabilities. This awareness is the first step toward avoiding such blunders, and if you've ever wondered about why you do what you do, the chances are you've developed such awareness and are unlikely to find yourself in prison smelling like a lemon orchard. Yet to truly excel and avoid the pitfalls of overconfidence or under-estimation of your abilities, merely recognising your actions and their outcomes isn't enough. You must elevate your self-awareness to the next level through metacognition, which means the practice of thinking about our thinking.

This extends beyond mere reflection on our actions, thoughts and emotions. It involves a deliberate effort to analyse and improve the way we process information, make decisions and learn from our experiences. For instance, consider the feedback I once received, likening my contributions in meetings to the presence of Darth Vader. It wasn't about heavy breathing or a penchant for global domination, but rather how my assertive delivery of ideas could unintentionally overshadow and intimidate. This moment of reflection wasn't just enlightening; it was a call to action, urging me to embrace a different approach – 'powerless communication', which Adam Grant advocates. This strategy, which I'll delve into in Chapter 5, increased my influence, ensuring my voice enhanced discussions rather than silencing them.

This shift didn't just alter my meeting dynamics; it was a metacognitive journey from being the unintentional Darth Vader of conference rooms to becoming a more inclusive and effective communicator. It illustrates the power of metacognition; by critically examining your thinking and behaviour, you can transform your interactions and relationships.

Minding the stimulus–response gap

Every day, we all navigate a world brimming with stimuli, eliciting a wide range of reactions. Some are instinctual, such as the reflexive jerk of a hand away from a scalding surface, while others only appear instinctive, such as the things we say in the heat of the moment. Then there are moments that demand our full attention, such as crafting our words carefully in a sensitive conversation or making a significant decision. Importantly, beyond the realm of automatic reactions lies the opportunity to choose how we respond.

As we're reminded by Transport for London, we can 'mind the gap'. Victor Frankl, Holocaust survivor and author of *Man's Search for Meaning* (1946, translated 1959), profoundly stated: 'Between stimulus and response, there is a space. In that space lies our freedom and our power to choose our response. In our response lies our growth and our happiness.' (Pattakos & Covey 2010) If Frankl could sustain this belief amid the horrors of the Holocaust, it's clear that this mindset is attainable for us all, regardless of our individual circumstances.

Our sense of control over what happens in our lives, which is often explored in psychological research, is known as our locus of control (Rotter 1966). In other words, it's about whether we believe we're at the mercy of external forces or if we think we have the power to shape our outcomes. Everyone falls somewhere between two extremes – an external locus of control, feeling as if life's events are out of our hands; and an internal locus of control, the belief that we can influence our destiny through our actions. This difference can play out in many situations – for instance, believing you were rejected for a job because of your lack of preparation or because the hiring manager was biased.

One of the most powerful embodiments of an internal locus of control is immortalised in the 1875 poem 'Invictus' by William Ernest Henley. Crafted while Henley was recovering from multiple surgeries, this poem was frequently recited by Nelson Mandela during his incarceration. In the final verse, Henley states, 'It matters not how strait the gate, how charged with punishments the scroll, I am the master of my fate, I am the captain of my soul.' J R R Tolkien also advises this in *The Fellowship of the Ring* (1954), where Gandalf counsels Frodo, 'All we have to decide is what do with the time that is given to us.'

Like many great ideas, this one has been around for a while, and its roots can be traced back to Roman times when the philosopher Seneca observed, 'Luck is what happens when preparation meets opportunity.' This enduring sentiment, echoing through different cultures and time periods, underscores the empowering essence of developing an internal locus of control. This idea is frequently discussed on *The High Performance Podcast*. The presenters, Damian Hughes and Jake Humphrey, frame this in terms of fault versus responsibility, arguing that while many things in our lives may not be our fault, it's our responsibility to respond to them. The podcast provides numerous examples of people living a life of total responsibility, a characteristic frequently observed among high performers.

The perfect example of this mindset is encapsulated in the extraordinary journey of Billy Monger. A British racing driver, Billy had a life that was far from ordinary, defined not by tragedy but by his tenacious spirit. At just 17 years old and teetering on the brink of a professional racing career, Billy's life took a severe detour. He was involved in a horrific accident, a crash of such magnitude that he awoke to the stark reality of having both his legs amputated. Instead of gearing up for the racetracks, Billy found himself spending his 18th birthday in a hospital bed, a moment that could easily have signalled the end of his racing dreams. But the spirit of a true racer is not easily extinguished. Displaying a resilience that defies belief, Billy was back behind the wheel merely 11 weeks later, the hospital corridors replaced by the familiar embrace of the racing circuit. His determination didn't stop at simply getting back in the car. Billy went on to compete in the high-stakes world of Formula 4 and 3 racing, his story a testament to the triumph of the human spirit over adversity. His journey reminds us that external circumstances may shape our lives, but it's our response that truly defines us.

You can hear more about Billy's journey in his interview on *The High Performance Podcast* (Humphrey & Hughes Nov 2020). In it, he reflects on the mental strength he's developed since the accident and shares his new-found perspective on taking personal responsibility and overcoming obstacles. He also reveals an impressive ability to deal with trivial things quickly and embrace his shortcomings, focusing on ways to improve rather than resorting to blame games when things don't go as planned. His story is an inspiring testament to the power of resilience and personal responsibility in the face of adversity.

Moving from the racetrack to the peaks of the world's highest mountains, we find another embodiment of this mindset in Nims Purja. Known for holding multiple mountaineering records, an epic story he tells in his 2020 book *Beyond Possible* (also a film on Netflix, *14 Peaks: Nothing Is Impossible*), Nims is no stranger to adversity and the power of personal choice in the face of seemingly impossible odds. One example stands out during his journey trying to shatter the world record for climbing Everest, Lhotse and Makalu. High in the unforgiving terrain of Camp Four, aptly named the death zone, Nims found his oxygen supply had been stolen. Here, in the most serious of situations, it would've been easy to give in to anger and blame. However, Nims opted for a different approach. He chose to imagine a scenario in which his stolen oxygen was used in an emergency, potentially saving someone's life. This perspective, even if untrue, provided him with a sense of happiness and renewed energy to keep going (Purja 2020). Just as with Billy, and regardless of whether you agree with the decision he made, Nims' story is a perfect example of the power of choosing our response in the most trying of circumstances.

Balancing control and acceptance

While wishing to live a life of total responsibility and developing a locus of control are great aspirations, it's vital that this pursuit doesn't morph into an unhealthy and damaging obsession. It's essential to understand that this mindset isn't about assuming blame for situations outside your control. It's not your fault when others act inappropriately, nor should you shoulder the weight of the world to the detriment of your mental health. The objective of this mindset is to recognise that while many things may not be your fault, it's within your capacity, and therefore your responsibility, to determine how you'll respond to them. It's an idea encapsulated by Reinhold Niebuhr's 'Serenity Prayer': 'God grant me the serenity to accept the things I cannot change, the courage to change the things I can, and the wisdom to know the difference.' It's about harnessing your inner strength to navigate the challenges of life rather than playing the victim and being overwhelmed by them.

Sometimes individuals can get stuck in a victim mentality, a mindset that sharply contrasts with the intentionality I've explored so far. As highlighted earlier, we all exist on a spectrum when it comes to our locus of control, with intentionality positioned at one end and learned helplessness at the other. Positive psychologist Martin Seligman coined the term to describe the mindset of dogs that resigned themselves to endure escapable shocks after being subjected to inescapable ones (Seligman 1972). Learned helplessness isn't exclusive to animals; humans can fall into this pattern as well, leading to the belief that we're powerless to effect change in our own lives. You might recognise these beliefs in people you know, or even yourself, hearing things such as 'Why does this always happen to me?', 'I'm rubbish at things like that' or 'I never get anything right'. Children who struggle academically are particularly vulnerable to developing learned helplessness, as they may start to perceive their efforts as ineffective and consequently not worth their time.

The good news is that no one is born with the belief that they can't control their surroundings and it's pointless to try. This is precisely why it's termed 'learned' helplessness, underscoring the potential for a different behaviour to be developed. This new learning is the very start of the development journey towards intentionality – a journey that's beneficial for us all, as the rewards include improved decision making, enhanced happiness, increased self-efficacy, greater effectiveness, higher achievement, resilience and improved leadership effectiveness.

The power of language

The language you use significantly impacts your capacity for intentionality. One impactful linguistic change I've adopted is refusing to say 'I'm too busy', instead replacing it with 'That's not a priority for me'. In our daily lives, it's not a case of being too busy, but rather of setting priorities – and this shift from external, reactive thinking to internal, proactive thinking is empowering. Openly declaring that something isn't a priority also prompts the consideration of whether it should be. While setting priorities is something to consider in professional settings, it's equally effective in your personal life. Try it out when you're struggling to find time for a date night, seeing friends or spending time with your family.

During a recent business strategy meeting, one of my team members expressed discomfort about using this phrase. However, this discomfort is precisely the point; it urges us to be intentional with our time. On a similar note, banning the word 'should' in our household has been liberating, allowing us to focus on the things we want or need to do. I guarantee you that applying these principles will make a significant difference to your life, making you more effective and ensuring that you give yourself and your relationships the respect they deserve.

Captain L David Marquet offers another potent example of the power of language in his book *Turn the Ship Around* (2013). He transformed the worst-performing submarine crew in the US Navy into the best in the fleet, and one of the key ways in which he did this was by encouraging proactive language. Instead of asking senior officers what they should do, he encouraged individuals to adopt the phrase 'I intend to do x' and confirmed they were OK to proceed (Marquet 2013). This approach transformed the mindset of all on board, resulting in individuals taking ownership and thinking in a more proactive way, which was instrumental in creating a high-performance culture. While you may not be on a submarine, this linguistic shift is something you can adopt into your daily language and will deliver impressive results.

These examples underline the significance of taking responsibility for your self-talk, something that's critical in developing an internal locus of control. Recognising and combating negative self-talk is vital in overcoming learned helplessness and is a vital step in the journey towards intentionality. If negative self-talk is a significant issue for you, seeking guidance from a mentor or coach is something you'll benefit from.

Managing your response

One particular point that has stirred much debate over the years, yet one that I fervently stand by, is the notion that we have the power to choose our response in any given situation. Sometimes we choose badly, and sometimes we may not even be aware we've chosen, but we do choose. We choose when we react emotionally to our partners, we choose when we 'say something without thinking', we choose when we act on impulse, and we choose when we fire off a quick email or text.

Regarding emotional responses, it's pertinent to note that while your initial emotional reaction might be spontaneous, the intensity of your emotions is shaped by your beliefs and the choices you make in responding to situations. This principle is captured in the Buddhist parable of the 'second arrow' (Brach 2013). Buddha once asked a student, 'If a person is struck by an arrow, is it painful? If the person is struck by a second arrow, is it even more painful?' The Buddha goes on to explain that in life we can't always control the first arrow, but the second arrow is our reaction to the first, and that arrow we can control. It's this second arrow that represents the beliefs we hold, the thoughts and stories we tell ourselves and the way we speak to ourselves, which in turn inform how painfully we experience the initial event.

For instance, if you experience rejection, the initial disappointment is the first arrow, beyond your control. However, if you then berate yourself, deeming yourself a failure and giving airtime to the belief that you'll always fail, you deepen your pain. This reaction constitutes the second arrow. This concept is also the central premise of rational emotive behaviour therapy, which proposes that you become upset not because of the events taking place in your life but rather your beliefs about these events (Ross 2006).

The circles of control, influence and acceptance

The essence of making wise choices and living intentionally hinges on your ability to direct your energies appropriately towards the challenges and opportunities you face. Stephen Covey (2020) presents a powerful framework to guide this process, conceptualised as three concentric circles: the circle of control, the circle of influence and the circle of concern.

At the heart of this framework is the circle of control, encompassing those aspects of your life over which you have direct power, the decisions you make, your responses to others and your personal attitudes. When faced with a situation, asking 'Can I control it?' helps you identify if it falls within this circle.

Surrounding this is the circle of influence, which includes elements you can affect but not control outright. These might be the attitudes of friends or trends in your workplace. To determine if a stimulus belongs here, you ask 'Can I influence it?'

Finally, the outermost circle of concern holds those issues that impact you but lie beyond your control or influence, such as global economic trends, natural disasters or the actions of distant governments. Here, the critical question becomes, 'Can I accept it?'. If you find acceptance challenging, it prompts you to reassess, exploring if there's a way to move the issue into your circle of influence, or ultimately to cultivate acceptance and peace with the situation as is.

To illustrate, I found these questions invaluable in handling my responses to an individual who's consistently self-absorbed, rarely showing interest in anyone else. This led to many one-sided conversations and a great deal of frustration. First, I questioned if I could control the person's behaviour. Since you can't dictate another person's actions, I ruled this out. Next, I considered the possibility of influencing their actions. I realised this might be possible but would involve no small effort on my part and could potentially put a considerable strain on the relationship, a price I wasn't willing to pay. Finally, I asked myself if I could accept their behaviour. This time, the answer was yes, and I decided to adjust my expectations, adopting a mindset of not getting angry at people for behaving the way they always behave. Without any change in the other person's behaviour, my emotional response to our interactions dramatically improved, demonstrating the power of this shift in perspective. This approach has proved effective time and again.

On a wider scale, the Covid-19 pandemic served as a global experiment, testing how nations and individuals respond to the same stimulus in the absence of pre-existing guidance on how to behave. Almost overnight, a significant proportion of the global workforce found themselves transitioning to working from home, a circumstance initially expected to last for only three weeks. This situation was unprecedented as, although distributed work has been a part of the professional landscape for years, it had never been adopted on such an enormous scale.

For those who lived through this period, it became glaringly obvious that the initial novelty of working from home quickly wore off for many, as the restrictions on normal activities began to weigh heavily. However, those who swiftly established new routines, dressed for work instead of remaining in their pyjamas and proactively took control of their situation fared much better. I observed that clients, colleagues and friends who embraced this proactive mindset throughout the pandemic were not only happier and more productive but also enjoyed better mental health.

While there are numerous other examples I could present, the key takeaway from this chapter is that being intentional can be applied to nearly every stimulus in your daily life. In essence, what matters most is not what you experience in life, but how you respond to those experiences.

Application
Turning principles into practice

Increase your self-awareness

Improving self-awareness requires investing time in reflecting on your thoughts, feelings and actions. Reflective practice can be a valuable tool to help you do this. To engage with reflective practice, it's beneficial to analyse recent situations, considering your thoughts, feelings, the consequences, what you have learned as a result and what you can do differently next time, by asking yourself the following three questions:

+ What?
+ So what?
+ What next?

Dedicating regular time for self-reflection is key, whether daily, weekly or after significant events. Some people might find journaling helpful, while others might prefer discussing their thoughts and experiences with a trusted friend, colleague, partner or mentor.

To maximise the benefit from doing this, focus on stimuli within your circle of control or influence, and try to empathise with others involved in the situation. Write down your insights and, most importantly, your plans for future action. This enables you to review and hold yourself accountable for your development over time.

Develop an internal locus of control

To cultivate an internal locus of control, instead of blaming others or external factors, start by taking responsibility for your actions. When events occur, work backwards to identify the factors within your control or influence to understand your contribution and opportunities for potential improvements. Pay attention to the language you and others use and be mindful of reactive phrases such as 'That's just the way I am' or 'I can't help it'. The intent here is not to berate yourself for using this language, but to identify opportunities to change your language and consequently your mindset. Getting feedback from those around you can also be beneficial here.

Widen the gap

Like any other skill, improving intentionality requires practice. Mentally rehearse or visualise responding to stimuli ahead of time in preparation for the real thing. Work through the circles of control, influence and acceptance model, considering your options for responding, weighing the pros and cons, and decide on your course of action. Make a habit of reflecting after such encounters, celebrating your wins and holding yourself accountable for any setbacks.

As well as negative self-talk, you may also have negative limiting beliefs: false things you tell yourself that hold you back from taking responsibility and being intentional in your life. These negative limiting beliefs typically come in three forms: beliefs about you, beliefs about the world and beliefs about life. Perpetuating these beliefs is a sure-fire way to operate as your inner critic rather than your inner cheerleader. One of the most effective ways to widen the stimulus–response gap is to address your limiting beliefs, and a great way to do this is to work through Dr Albert Ellis's ABCDE model (1991):

A **activating event** – an event triggers a problem for you
B **beliefs** – your interpretations or thoughts about the situation
C **consequences** – the outcomes of your beliefs, which may include emotional, behavioural and physical reactions
D **disputing beliefs** – the process of questioning and challenging irrational or unreasonable beliefs and replacing unhelpful thoughts with more constructive, rational ones

E **effective behaviour** – the stage where we align our actions with our new beliefs, leading to improved behaviours and outcomes.

For instance, if asked to give a presentation at work, you might initially believe you'll forget your material, fail and embarrass yourself. This belief could lead to consequences such as feeling nauseous, sweaty palms, dread and attempts to avoid the situation. However, the true strength of the ABCDE model lies in its ability to reframe your perspective. You can choose to believe you have plenty of time to prepare, that detailed notes will guide your talk, that previous successes prove your capabilities and that your audience is supportive. These new, positive beliefs can calm you and equip you to deliver a successful presentation.

A – activating event

+ What is the activating event?
+ What happened?
+ What did I do?
+ What did others do?
+ What was I thinking at the time?
+ What was I feeling at the time?

B – beliefs

+ What do I believe because of the event?
+ Which of these beliefs are helpful?
+ Which of these beliefs are unhelpful?
+ What assumptions am I making?

C – consequences

+ What am I feeling now?
+ What did I do as a result?
+ Is my behaviour consistent with how I want to behave?
+ Am I proud of how I behaved?

D – dispute

+ What would I say to a close friend who shared that belief?
+ What evidence do I have for my beliefs?
+ In what ways is my belief helpful or unhelpful?
+ What more helpful beliefs can I use to replace the unhelpful beliefs?

E – effective behaviour

+ What are the results of my new behaviour?
+ How do I behave this way consistently?
+ Who can hold me accountable for this?

Grow your circle

Those who master the art of being intentional often foresee situations occurring and respond proactively, mitigating the emotional intensity of the stimuli. To operate at this level, review your personal and professional life to identify opportunities for proactive action to achieve better outcomes.

A simple but powerful way of applying Covey's circle model, either by yourself or with a team, is to follow these steps:

+ Draw out the three circles (concern, influence and control) on a large piece of paper or a digital platform.
+ Write down all the stimuli you're facing on sticky notes and put them in the corresponding circle.
+ If you're working with a team, discuss your placement of each item. If working individually, reflect on your placements.
+ For everything in your circle of concern, identify ways to influence or control them and move these items into the appropriate circle.
+ Develop a plan to implement the actions required to make these changes.

Key takeaways

→ There's a gap between a stimulus, an event or circumstance and your response to it.

→ The essence of intentionality rests in broadening this gap and choosing your responses.

→ A fundamental component of this is developing an internal locus of control: the belief that you're in control of your life.

→ Your language plays a significant role in shaping your mindset and determining your ability to act intentionally.

→ You need to focus your energy on what lies within your circles of control and influence and try to accept what's outside of these.

Go deeper

→ *The 7 Habits of Highly Effective People*, Stephen Covey

→ Billy Monger, *The High Performance Podcast*

→ Nims Purja, *The High Performance Podcast*

→ *High Performance*, Jake Humphrey and Damian Hughes

→ *Man's Search for Meaning*, Victor Frankl

Chapter 5
Align your decisions

Make better decisions by being aware of biases, gaining perspective, following a robust process and considering appropriate options.

How we make decisions

Our world has been significantly shaped by a series of pivotal decisions – some good, some disastrously bad. Consider those who refused to publish the Harry Potter series, the initial rejection of the Beatles and the insufficient lifeboats on the Titanic. These incidents highlight not just missed opportunities and financial blunders but also the devastating impact of flawed decision making. Each of us makes a vast number of decisions every day, varying in significance. As John C Maxwell (2007), a distinguished leadership author, insightfully notes: 'Life is a matter of choices, and every choice you make makes you.'

Understanding how you make decisions is crucial to improving them. Daniel Kahneman, a Nobel Prize-winning psychologist and author of *Thinking, Fast and Slow* (2012), dedicated his life to this study. He describes two decision-making systems: System 1, which operates quickly and automatically with minimal effort; and System 2, which is slower, deliberate and requires more effort and control. Like water seeking the path of least resistance, we often opt for the easier route in decision making. This tendency can lead us to rely on gut feelings or readily available information, a mental shortcut. While these shortcuts are often helpful, they can also lead to significant errors, particularly when we're unaware of their influence.

The notion that our decisions are entirely rational is challenged by the field of behavioural economics. In *Predictably Irrational* (2009), Dan Ariely, professor of psychology and behavioural economics, demonstrates how our decisions are heavily influenced by external factors, emotions and our desire for social acceptance (Grant 2014). However, that doesn't mean we're powerless bystanders. In fact, understanding how we make decisions and recognising that this process requires effort and attention is the first step towards taking ownership. The goal isn't to eliminate System 1 thinking but to discern when System 2's deliberate approach is necessary, such as in high-stake situations or when the likelihood of error is high. For instance, System 1 is totally capable of helping us walk home along a familiar route, whereas we need System 2 to help us explore a brand new place on holiday.

A perspective on decision making

Perspective is a pivotal factor in the decision-making process. Consider loss aversion, for instance. This describes how people typically perceive the sting of losses more acutely than the joy of gains. This tendency leads us to prioritise avoiding losses over pursuing potential benefits. It also gives rise to the 'sunk cost fallacy', where we continue investing in a failing project, enduring an unsatisfying job or persisting with a book we're not enjoying simply because we've already invested time or resources in it (Kahneman 2012, Grant 2014).

Your attitude towards risk is significantly shaped by the context of a litigious society, where the default often leans towards the safety of the familiar. This cautious stance is rooted in the belief that sticking to standard processes carries less risk, buoyed by the adage that no one has been fired for doing what they've always done. Yet this approach can inadvertently dampen the pursuit of innovative decisions that might yield better outcomes. Cultivating a culture that marries accountability with a non-punitive stance is crucial for fostering continuous improvement. Such an environment not only facilitates more effective decision making but also highlights the critical role of psychological safety, essential for enhancing wellbeing.

Your perspectives shape your decisions in several other ways. For instance, your responses differ when operating under social norms versus market norms. You might help a friend move house for a simple thank you or a takeout (social norm), but would feel undervalued if offered an equivalent payment for the same task (market norm). Even the image you wish to project influences your decisions, such as what you choose to eat or drink in a social setting, a factor that's more influential than you might think. Moreover, your decisions tend to lean towards honesty when reminded of ethical standards, such as recalling the Ten Commandments or signing an honour code, even if the code itself is fictitious (Ariely 2009).

Finally, your role as a buyer or seller profoundly affects your perspective during transactions. Sellers frequently focus on their emotional attachment and losing the item's sentimental value, while buyers view the exchange more objectively as a potential gain, and are more critical of flaws. This contrast underlines the concept that the value of an item is determined more by what someone is willing to pay for it than by the seller's perception of it.

Why we make bad decisions

Poor decision making often stems from four key factors:

+ cognitive distortions – our minds convincing us of untruths
+ cognitive biases – systematic errors in our thinking

+ processing errors – flawed approaches in decision making
+ logical fallacies – errors in logical arguments.

This chapter will focus on the first three, as avoiding logical fallacies primarily involves increasing our understanding of the subject at hand.

Cognitive distortions

Addressing cognitive distortions is central to most cognitive behavioural therapeutic (CBT) interventions. This involves identifying and challenging the false narratives our minds create, enabling us to reject them and make better decisions for more fulfilling lives (Beck 1991; Burns 1980). Some common cognitive distortions that influence our decision making include the following.

→ **Filtering:** Focusing only on the negative aspects of a situation while ignoring positive ones. For instance, receiving feedback on a piece of work that's mostly positive with some constructive criticism. Filtering would lead you to focus only on the criticism, overlooking the positive comments and concluding the work was a failure.

→ **Polarised thinking:** Oversimplifying situations, leaving no room for complexity or middle ground. For instance, eating a slice of cake at a party and thinking it completely ruined your diet instead of seeing a diet as a balance of healthy eating with occasional treats.

→ **Overgeneralisation:** Using a single instance as evidence of a broader pattern. For instance, concluding that no one will ever be interested in you based on one experience of someone not replying following a date.

→ **Jumping to conclusions or catastrophising:** Assuming the worst outcome without sufficient evidence. For instance, concluding you must have offended your boss and are going to get fired just because they haven't quickly replied to your email, even though there's no evidence to support this.

➜ **Always being right**: Prioritising being right over the feelings of others. For instance, refusing to acknowledge your friend's viewpoint, insisting you're right and putting strain on the relationship.

Cognitive biases

Distinct from cognitive distortions, cognitive biases are systematic errors in our thinking that significantly influence decision making. Unlike distortions, which are false beliefs, biases are more about misjudgement and flawed reasoning. The 'Cognitive Bias Codex' by John Manoogian, available on Wikimedia, illustrates the extensive range of cognitive biases, whereas this chapter will focus on a few prevalent ones that impact decision making: anchoring bias, confirmation bias, optimism bias and overconfidence bias.

➜ **Anchoring bias**: Consider two people who buy the same shirt for £60. One sees it reduced from £100, while the other only sees the £60 price tag. The person who experiences the reduction from £100 is likely to feel more satisfied with the purchase. This illustrates the anchoring effect, where an initial value influences our perception of worth. It's a robust effect in psychology, influencing decisions from house buying to salary negotiations (Kahneman 2012). In marketing, this is exploited through the 'decoy effect' where the presence of a higher-priced item increases the sales of the second most expensive option (Ariely 2009). Just think about how often you've ordered the mid-price steak or wine, or a medium coffee.

➜ **Confirmation bias**: One of the most challenging biases in decision making is confirmation bias. This involves focusing on information that supports your pre-existing beliefs, ignoring contradictory evidence. This bias is particularly problematic because you might believe you're doing thorough research when, in fact, you're only considering information that aligns with your existing views. This is exacerbated by the algorithms behind search engines and social media, which tend to show you what they think you want to see (Kahneman 2012; Ariely 2009; Heath & Heath 2014). In summing up confirmation bias, the conclusion comes first and the supporting evidence follows.

→ **Optimism bias**: Optimism bias leads us to overestimate our chances of success, often neglecting evidence from similar situations. Daniel Kahneman describes this as focusing on the 'inside view' and advises adopting an 'outside view' for a more balanced perspective, a technique known as 'reference class forecasting'. While optimism is valuable, it's crucial to balance it with realistic assessments of potential outcomes.

→ **Overconfidence bias**: Many people, especially experts, exhibit overconfidence bias, placing too much trust in their abilities and predictions about the future (Kahneman 2012; Heath & Heath 2014). This bias is evident in the fact that most people consider themselves above-average drivers and that most university professors rate themselves as superior teachers, despite neither being mathematically possible (Alicke & Govorun 2005; Svenson 1981; Cross 1977). While confidence in one's abilities is important, the unpredictable nature of the future and the presence of 'unknown unknowns' should temper overconfidence. You therefore need to be careful about relying on intuition unless you're in stable, predictable environments (Heath & Heath 2014).

Processing errors

In addition to cognitive distortion and biases, our decision making is often hindered by processing errors. These don't necessarily influence what we decide, but rather how we decide, leading to a less effective decision-making process. The main processing errors include emotional influence, decision fatigue and the handling of options.

➜ **Emotion:** Emotions, especially short-term ones, can significantly influence your decisions, often negatively. Surprised by the reckless sexual behaviour of others and think you'd be more sensible? You may be surprised, as the outcome of a study finding students in a non-aroused state were unable to accurately predict their decisions in an aroused state, often underestimating the influence of passion (Ariely 2009). This suggests a Dr Jekyll and Mr Hyde effect, where your emotional state can lead you to make decisions your rational self might not recognise.

➜ **Decision fatigue:** This occurs when the effort of decision making exhausts your mental resources, leading to poor choices. To conserve energy, your brain might not fully engage in thoughtful decision making. Barack Obama exemplified a strategy to combat this: by limiting his choices in clothing and food, he conserved his decision-making energy for more important matters (Lewis 2012). This example highlights the importance of recognising when you're mentally drained and making allowances for this state (Kahneman 2012).

The impact of options

How you handle options can also lead to processing errors. Narrow framing limits you to a few options, often creating a binary either/or situation. An episode of the sitcom *The Big Bang Theory* demonstrates this: a character is torn between a job offer from an ex-boyfriend that would make her husband uncomfortable and staying in an unfulfilling job. An argument ensues, with both characters fixated on the two options, failing to consider the multitude of other employment opportunities that are potentially available. Admittedly, exploring these other options would've made for less dramatic television, but it's a classic case of the impact of narrow framing.

On the flip side, keeping too many options open and attempting to engage in every opportunity or interest that comes your way can also be a trap. This desire to participate in everything you want to can lead you to spread yourself too thin. This overextension not only diminishes your effectiveness in these pursuits but also risks the quality of your connections with family and friends. It's necessary to remember that inaction or reluctance to prioritise is a choice to persist with the status quo. By not actively choosing what truly merits your time and energy, you inadvertently allow valuable aspects of your life to slip through the cracks, underscoring the importance of thoughtful selection and commitment.

Mastering the art of decision making

Being aware of your biases, distortions and processing errors is the first step in mitigating their impact. Making sound decisions often involves engaging Kahneman's System 2, your slower, more deliberate thinking process, and this means acknowledging that good decision making takes effort. Therefore, you should aim to make key decisions when you have the energy to do so, or postpone them to a time when you can fully engage your cognitive resources.

Understanding the role of emotions in your decision making is also crucial. You should avoid making significant decisions during times of high emotion, delaying them until you can approach the situation rationally. Another approach is to visualise how you'll feel about a decision in the future; for instance, how the choice you make will feel a week, a month or even a year from now. To address cognitive distortions, you could turn to the ABCDE model proposed by Dr Albert Ellis, as discussed in Chapter 4, to help reframe and rationalise your thoughts.

Furthermore, defining key priorities in life can help in decision making. Asking yourself 'If I decide to do this, what else must stop?' is a question that can bring clarity to tough decisions. This approach ensures your decisions align not only with your immediate desires but also your long-term goals and vision for life.

In addition to these general principles, there are some specific techniques you can use to enhance your decision making.

➔ **Thinking 'and' instead of 'or'**: When faced with a decision that seems to have only two options, challenge yourself to think beyond the apparent options. Asking what else you could do if the current options weren't available can unlock alternative solutions. It's also beneficial to seek insight from others who have faced similar dilemmas, though you must be wary of decision paralysis, getting stuck in the option generation phase and never moving forward (Heath & Heath 2014).

➔ **Asking the right question**: Often, people fixate on a decision without considering if they're addressing the right issue. This typically happens when they get stuck in the weeds and lose sight of what they're trying to achieve. By stepping back and focusing on your ultimate goal, you can uncover options that align more closely with your objectives. This approach can help with decisions as major as job changes, such as whether the additional salary is worth the extra commute, and the more minor, such as designing the layout of home furniture.

➜ **Get some perspective**: Try looking at your situation as an outsider would. What advice would you give a friend facing the same decision? Business leaders, for instance, can consider what a successor might do in their position, obtaining a viewpoint unencumbered by the sunk cost fallacy. Another technique is to 'consider the opposite', challenging yourself to think about what would happen if the reverse of your current thinking were true. Creativity expert Michael Michalko suggests taking this further by reversing the core assumptions of any proposal to explore alternative solutions (Syed 2021). For instance, by reversing the core assumption that a taxi company must own their own cars, we ended up with Uber.

➜ **Seek out disagreement**: It's comfortable to surround yourself with agreement, but this can reinforce confirmation bias. To counteract this, you need to create an environment where dissent isn't just allowed but encouraged. Often, when you seek feedback, you unconsciously want affirmation rather than honest critique. Instead of presenting ideas with passion and then asking for opinions, you'll benefit from engaging in what's known as 'powerless communication'. This involves asking questions that elicit balanced views and demonstrate your openness to different opinions. Questions such as 'Why won't this work?', 'Why is this a bad idea?' and 'What am I missing?' can be instrumental in revealing valuable insights and perspective that you might otherwise miss.

➜ **Test don't guess**: Implement the principle of testing ideas on a small scale before fully committing. This agile approach, applicable in various areas of life, allows you to gather real-world data and make informed decisions. It's relevant to many life decisions, such as renting in an area before buying property, or gaining work experience before fully committing to a career in that profession. Even in your romantic life, you'll instinctively follow this approach by dating someone before deciding on a lifelong commitment such as marriage. This principle of 'testing the waters' can lead to more informed, confident and ultimately successful decisions in all areas of your life.

The role of tripwires

The essence of the 'test don't guess' approach is to 'fail fast', to quickly recognise when a path isn't working before investing too much time or resources. It's also invaluable for testing underlying assumptions that your decisions depend on. However, this approach has its risks, notably the sunk cost fallacy. You might reach a point where you should 'fail fast' yet feel compelled to continue due to your initial investment. This is where setting tripwires can be beneficial. Tripwires are pre-determined points that trigger a re-evaluation of the decision or project.

An iconic example of a tripwire in action is the rock band Van Halen's infamous brown M&Ms clause. Far from being an indication of overdemanding, entitled rock stars, this clause served as a simple yet effective safety check. The band required a bowl of M&Ms backstage, with the brown ones removed. If the band found brown M&Ms, it indicated that their detailed set-up instructions might not have been closely followed, potentially compromising their performance and safety. Failure of this simple test indicated the band needed to check every aspect of the remaining instructions.

In your own decision making, setting similar tripwires – clear indicators or milestones at which you reassess your path – can prevent you from falling prey to the sunk cost fallacy. These could range from time-bound reviews in a project to specific, measurable outcomes in personal goals such as the amount of money you'd spend on an investment.

For instance, while planning our wedding, my wife and I implemented a tripwire that any spend exceeding £100 required an agreement from both of us. This decision wasn't about exerting control over each other's spending; rather, it was a strategy to ensure that neither of us felt pressured into making hasty decisions by vendors, friends or family in the absence of the other. This approach effectively allowed us to pause, reflect and make joint decisions, reinforcing our partnership and shared responsibility in the planning process.

Follow the process

Enhancing our decision-making effectiveness significantly hinges on establishing and adhering to a robust process. While it's impractical to apply this rigour to every decision, it's invaluable for the more significant choices.

Firefighter, psychologist and author Sabrina Cohen-Hatton and psychologist Rob Honey developed a simple yet powerful approach known as 'decision controls'. Originally conceived for rapid decision making in high-stress scenarios, it's equally applicable in everyday contexts (Cohen-Hatton & Honey 2015). This model prompts you to consider three key questions.

→ **What am I trying to achieve?** This question helps to clarify the objective of the decision, ensuring the goal is well defined and focused.
→ **What do I expect to happen as a result?** This encourages you to think through the potential outcomes and consequences of your decision, fostering a forward-thinking mindset.
→ **Are the benefits worth the risks?** Here, you assess the balance between the possible rewards and inherent risks, allowing for a more calculated and informed decision.

Take, for instance, a business scenario where a team is considering launching a new product. By applying these decision controls, the team can analyse their project's objectives, consider the outcomes and weigh the potential risks against the anticipated rewards. Such structured thinking not only clarifies objectives but also mitigates the risk of unforeseen consequences.

Decision making in groups

Group dynamics significantly influence decision making, primarily through two mechanisms: hierarchical dominance and social conformity.

Hierarchical dominance occurs when the opinions of one or two individuals, often those in positions of authority or those who speak the most, inadvertently suppress other members' contributions. This phenomenon is sometimes referred to as the 'HiPPO (highest paid person's opinion) effect', where a group relies more on the opinion of the highest-paid individual rather than on data or insights from more junior, but possibly more knowledgeable, members. In extreme cases, such as in the airline industry, hierarchical dynamics can even lead to life-threatening situations, as there have been several examples of co-pilots dying rather than risking contradicting the captain (Syed 2021). Unfortunately, removing the leader from the room sometimes doesn't improve the decision making; it just creates a time delay while the leader's approval is sought, something General Stanley McChrystal reflects on in his book *Team of Teams* (2015).

In contrast, social conformity doesn't require any hierarchy. It stems from our innate need for belonging and fear of rejection by the group. Solomon Asch's experiments in the 1950s demonstrated that social pressure could lead people to give incorrect answers to simple questions, such as estimating the length of a line (Asch 1951). This tendency underlines the concept of 'groupthink', where the desire for group harmony overrides the pursuit of optimal decision making.

To counteract these influences, author Edward de Bono

proposed the 'six thinking hats' method, which assigns different thinking styles to six coloured hats: white for objective facts, red for emotions, black for identifying weaknesses, yellow for positivity, green for creative ideas and blue for process control. This approach encourages diverse thinking, allowing members to express concerns or emotions they might otherwise suppress. It also streamlines meetings, as each hat guides the group's focus, often leading to faster and more effective decision making (De Bono 1985).

Choice architecture and the psychology of nudges

Choice architecture refers to the process and context in which individuals make decisions. A key area of interest in behavioural economics, it examines how 'choice architects', those who design decision-making environments, can subtly influence individuals to make better choices. Central to this field is the concept of nudge theory, popularised by behavioural economist Richard Thaler and legal scholar Cass Sunstein (2022). Nudge theory suggests that small, subtle changes, or 'nudges', can significantly alter people's behaviour in a positive way without imposing controls. To be considered a nudge, these interventions must be easy and cheap to implement, as well as non-mandatory.

Numerous real-world examples illustrate the effectiveness of nudges. For instance, positioning fruit at eye level in shops, as opposed to unhealthy snacks, can nudge customers towards healthier eating choices. Similarly, the image of a fly etched in a urinal in public restrooms can improve aiming accuracy, thereby reducing cleaning costs. Another simple yet impactful nudge is the use of reminder texts for medical appointments, which has been shown to decrease no-show rates.

The success of nudge theory has led to the establishment of specialised 'nudge units' in governments around the world. These units apply behavioural insights to public policy, aiming to steer individuals towards better choices without removing their freedom to choose. In your own life you can think about how nudges could be applied in your own environment. Consider what small changes could be made to influence better decisions or behaviours, either in personal or professional contexts.

Application
Turning principles into practice

Avoiding decision fatigue

A crucial aspect of effective decision making is ensuring you're in the right mental state to make good choices. This primarily means avoiding decision fatigue, a state of mental exhaustion from making too many decisions. Decision fatigue can significantly impair judgement and make you prone to errors. Two effective ways to do this are as follows.

→ **Simplify daily choices:** One way to combat this is by simplifying your daily choices and limiting trivial ones. You can apply this principle in your own life by establishing routines that eliminate daily decisions. For instance, planning meals for the week not only helps with eating healthily and budgeting but also frees you from deciding what to cook each evening after a tiring day at work.

→ **Creating decision-making routines:** Another effective strategy is to create decision-making routines. This could involve designating specific times for certain types of decisions or batching similar decisions together to handle them more efficiently. By organising your decision-making process, you can ensure you tackle important choices when your energy and mental clarity are at their peak.

Consider the areas in your life where decision-making demands can be streamlined. Reducing the cognitive load from these smaller decisions can reserve your mental energy for the more significant choices, ultimately leading to better overall decision making.

Value-based decision making

One of the most straightforward yet powerful decision-making techniques involves aligning your choices with your purpose, values and priorities.

When faced with a decision, consider framing it in terms of the following questions:

+ Which outcome better aligns with my purpose?
+ Which outcome better aligns with my values?
+ Which outcome better aligns with my priorities?
+ If I say yes to this, what else am I saying no to?

For instance, consider what you would do if you were offered a lucrative job opportunity that required relocating to a city far from family and friends. Applying these questions, you might find that while the role aligns with your career priorities, it conflicts with personal values of family relationships and work–life balance. Such insights can guide you towards a decision that is consistent with your overall life vision.

Reflect on a recent decision you made. Apply these questions retrospectively to see how well the decision aligned with your values and purpose. This practice can illuminate the effectiveness of value-based decision making in everyday life.

Trust the process

When faced with decisions where a clear answer is elusive, it's crucial to have a robust and effective decision-making process. Sabrina Cohen-Hatton's 'Choice Controls' provide a solid foundation for this (Cohen-Hatton & Honey 2015):

→ What's my goal?
→ What do I expect to happen?
→ Is the benefit worth the risk?

These questions are vital in fast-paced situations, but you can adopt a similar approach for more complex decisions, integrating additional techniques within a three-stage framework.

Stage 1: Establish the goal

First, define what you aim to achieve with your decision. Avoid getting stuck in the detail and focus on your primary objective. Before exploring options, clearly outline your goal. Use the MoSCoW prioritisation method to establish what the ideal solution must, should, could and won't have. This approach helps you focus on essential requirements and avoid distractions.

For instance, when buying a house recently, the criteria my wife and I used were as follows:

+ must have: detached, garage, utility area
+ should have: west facing, large lounge
+ could have: integrated garage, log burner/fireplace.
+ won't have: three storeys.

Stage 2: Generate the options

Once your goal is set, list your options. As advocated by authors Chip and Dan Heath in Decisive (2014), think 'and' not 'or', and make sure you explore multiple possibilities. Aim for three to five viable options, avoiding the trap of too many choices that can lead to decision paralysis. Remember to consider the perspectives of others, seeking out other opinions or at least asking yourself what advice you would give to a friend or colleague in your situation. Remember to stay in the option generation phase without jumping to evaluate each option prematurely. This will help you, and anyone else involved, work with creative momentum.

Stage 3: Evaluate the options

With a shortlist of options, it's time for evaluation. To avoid biases in group settings, separate the idea from the person who generated it. This can be as simple as asking the same person to read out all the options, typing them up or asking different people to make the case for each option.

Consider the pros and cons, perform cost–benefit analyses and factor in effort and impact. Trusting your gut is valid but ensure it's not your sole decision criterion. Use the pre-mortem technique to foresee potential pitfalls (Klein 2007). This involves imagining a scenario where the option fails and identifying possible causes. This is an effective technique for identifying risks and can be used to inform your decision making.

Remember, the goal is not to find a perfect solution but the best possible one under the circumstances. In difficult situations, it can often be the case that all you are left with is to decide which option is the least bad. It's also important not to waste time waiting for certainty: as Obama suggests, sometimes 51 per cent certainty is enough to decide. Establish tripwires such as financial limits or deadlines to prevent falling into the sunk cost fallacy.

Finally, assess the outcome of your decision. This retrospective analysis is pivotal for continuous improvement in your decision making. Reflect on both the outcome and the process, identifying areas for future refinement.

For additional resources and insights, visit Chip and Dan Heath's website at heathbrothers.com.

Final thought: decision making in groups

While the decision-making process above is applicable both individually and in groups, there are additional strategies you can employ to enhance the effectiveness of group decisions.

→ **Build psychological safety:** Creating an environment of psychological safety is crucial in groups. When individuals feel safe, they're more likely to contribute ideas and engage in constructive challenges, which are both essential for effective decision making.

→ **Create a thinking environment:** Nancy Klein's *Time to Think* (1999) provides techniques to enhance group thinking quality. For example, creating dedicated uninterrupted time for each member to speak can lead to more thoughtful contributions and innovative solutions.

→ **Use the thinking hats:** Edward de Bono's *Six Thinking Hats* (1985) method can significantly improve group decision making. This technique allows group members to explore problems from different perspectives, from factual analysis to creative thinking, ensuring a well-rounded discussion.

→ **Graded assertiveness:** This technique is particularly useful in hierarchical settings, providing a framework for escalating communication assertively. One approach uses the acronym PACE:

  + **Probe:** Starting with a non-confrontational approach to clarify the issue, eg 'I was looking at the project plan and I see we have two weeks to complete this task; can you help me understand how we arrived at this timeframe?'

  + **Alert:** If the issue isn't resolved or acknowledged, you alert the decision maker in a more direct way, eg 'I've been reviewing the tasks we need to complete, and I'm concerned two weeks might not be enough time to thoroughly test the product, which could result in problems down the line.'

  + **Challenge:** If the issue remains unaddressed, you escalate your assertiveness, openly challenging the plan or decision, eg 'I strongly believe we're setting ourselves up for failure here. Have we considered the risks involved?'

  + **Emergency:** As a last resort, if all else fails and the issue is critical, you make a final, clear assertion, eg 'I must insist we review the timeline as rushing this implementation poses a significant risk to the project and the company. We need to reconsider our approach immediately.'

In group settings, these techniques can foster a more collaborative and effective decision-making environment. By integrating these approaches, teams can navigate complex decisions more successfully, ensuring that diverse perspectives are considered and group dynamics are managed effectively. Reflect on how you might implement these strategies in your next group decision-making session to experience their transformative impact.

Key takeaways

→ Recognise that your decision making is often influenced by cognitive distortions, biases and processing errors, resulting in you being less rational than you may think.

→ Being aware of these influences and engaging in Kahneman's System 2 thinking is crucial for enhancing the quality of your decisions.

→ Actively seeking external perspectives and considering how others might approach the situation can significantly improve decision-making outcomes.

→ Implementing tripwires – predetermined checkpoints that serve as critical moments to reassess and adjust your course – can prevent costly mistakes.

→ For significant decisions, employing a systematic decision-making process, such as the decision controls framework, can lead to more informed and effective outcomes.

Go deeper

→ *Decisive*, Chip and Dan Heath
→ *Predictably Irrational*, Dan Ariely
→ *Black Box Thinking*, Matthew Syed
→ *Thinking, Fast and Slow*, Daniel Kahneman
→ *The Heat of the Moment*, Sabrina Cohen-Hatton
→ Sabrina Cohen-Hatton, *The High Performance Podcast*
→ *Nudge*, Richard Thaler and Cass Sunstein
→ *Six Thinking Hats*, Edward de Bono
→ 'How to rethink a bad decision', *WorkLife with Adam Grant*
→ 'Ethical fading with Lenny Wong', A *Bit of Optimism* (a podcast with Simon Sinek)

Chapter 6
Embrace high performance

Become a high performer by playing to your strengths, being gritty, embracing failure, mastering feedback and developing good habits. Engage in deliberate practice in whatever you pursue and find harmony between your pursuit of excellence and maintaining your health.

What is high performance?

What springs to mind when you think about high performers? Perhaps it's gold medallists, famous musicians, influential vloggers or entrepreneurs who've created ground-breaking companies. How about the single parent providing for their family in a cost-of-living crisis, the nurse delivering excellent care at the end of a long shift or the teacher managing a difficult classroom in the face of yet more budget cuts? True high performers are everywhere in our daily lives. This chapter aims to unravel the mystery of excellence, showing that with the right mindset and approach, high performance is within everyone's reach.

The talent myth

The 'iron law of Canadian hockey', discovered during a 1980s junior match, raised serious questions about the long-held belief in the all-conquering nature of natural-born talent. It revealed a startling trend: most elite players were born in the early months of the year. This wasn't a case of astrological influence but a simple consequence of the 1 January age cut-off in youth hockey. This cut-off meant that, when the trials came around, those born in January were competing against others up to 12 months younger than them. Far from being an isolated case, this pattern has also been found in other sports that stream by age, such as baseball and football, as well as in academic performance, something that's arguably even more troubling (Galdwell 2009; Grant Oct 2022).

While individuals often outgrow the age-related disparities seen in youth sports and academia, the early advantages and disadvantages can have lasting effects. This dynamic gives rise to the 'Matthew effect', a term coined by sociologists Robert Merton and Harriet Zuckerman, which illustrates how initial advantages can compound over time, akin to the principle of 'the rich get richer and the poor get poorer', as depicted in the biblical Parable of the Talents (Merton 1968). In sports, for instance, those selected early for their perceived talent receive superior coaching, more practice opportunities and access to better facilities. This early selection not only gives them a considerable advantage over their peers but can also lead to those perceived as 'less talented' dropping out, discouraged by a mistaken belief in their inherent inferiority. This creates a self-reinforcing cycle where the early 'chosen' ones get progressively better, not solely because of inherent talent, but due to accumulated advantages (Gladwell 2009).

Historically, society has glorified high achievers, often attributing their success to innate genius. The philosopher Nietzsche critiqued this 'cult of the genius', noting our tendency to marvel at natural talent as if it sprang from thin air, without considering the journey behind it (Duckworth 2016). Such idolisation can be demotivating, leading us to give up too soon if we don't see immediate success, potentially missing out on becoming high performers ourselves.

It's important to acknowledge that while our innate nature plays a role, it's more of a predisposition than a predetermined path, meaning that success is more likely when we align our efforts with our natural interests and strengths (Clear 2018). The key takeaway here is that everyone has the potential for excellence, given the right circumstances and opportunities. High performance, therefore, isn't about a genetic lottery but maximising what we have, wherever we are. 'Our potential is one thing; what we do with it is quite another.' (Duckworth 2016; Syed 2011)

Deliberate practice

The journey towards high performance is less about the amount of natural talent you possess and more about the nature of your practice. Central to this journey is Anders Ericsson's concept of 'deliberate practice'. This form of practice is not about repeating what you already know; instead, it's about stretching your skills, constantly pushing beyond your comfort zone (Ericsson et al 1993). It's this continuous effort to tackle challenges that are just out of reach and set new goals upon reaching them that transforms an individual into an expert (Syed 2011).

Research spanning various fields, from music to sport to chess, consistently reveals that mastery requires around 10,000 hours of deliberate practice. Take the case of Mozart, often cited as a natural genius. By the time he composed his first piece at age six, he'd accumulated approximately 3,500 hours of practice. His exceptionalism lies, therefore, not in some mystical talent but in his early start and the intensity of his practice. Child prodigies such as Mozart amaze us because we compare them to peers their age, not those who've put in comparable amounts of practice. Far from being outliers, they exemplify the 10,000-hour rule (Syed 2011).

However, it's an oversimplification to say that practice alone leads to mastery. In addition to the quality of practice, factors such as effective coaching, a supportive network and access to resources all play pivotal roles (Grant Oct 2022; Syed 2011). Equally important is motivation. Without the inner drive to excel, engaging in the rigorous demands of deliberate practice is unlikely. This highlights the importance of making learning enjoyable, especially for young learners, to cultivate a lifelong commitment to improvement.

In summary, it's not just about clocking up 10,000 hours. It's about how those hours are spent and deliberate practice, enabled by the right conditions and a network of support (Gladwell 2009).

High performance isn't a gift bestowed upon a chosen few; it's about how we cultivate a high-performance mindset geared towards continuous growth and relentless improvement.

Cultivating a high-performance mindset: six key principles

Principle 1: Play to your strengths

'Everyone is a genius. But if you judge a fish by its ability to climb a tree, it will live its whole life believing that it is stupid.' This adage, often mistakenly attributed to Einstein, perfectly captures the essence of playing to our strengths. This principle isn't about how clever we are in a general sense, but how we are clever in our unique ways, asking ourselves 'how am I clever?', rather than 'how clever am I?' (Gardner 1983). It's about identifying our strengths, honing them and applying them effectively, while partnering with others to complement areas where we're not as strong. Remember, something is only a weakness if it's a necessary skill you lack; otherwise, it's merely a non-talent (Buckingham & Clifton 2004). For instance, my non-talent for DIY only becomes a weakness when we have a leak coming through the kitchen ceiling...

Principle 2: Develop grit

Grit, the perseverance in pursuing long-term goals, has been identified as a more significant predictor of success than IQ. Having grit means maintaining focus on high-level objectives and steadily working towards smaller, incremental goals (Duckworth 2016). It's crucial, however, to recognise when it's wise to let go of a specific lesser goal that isn't serving your larger purpose, for instance stopping a project if it's not going to deliver the benefits you expected. True grit involves knowing when to persist and when to pivot, ensuring you're not doggedly following a path that leads away from your ultimate aims or a losing course of action (Whyte 1986).

Principle 3: Embrace failure

'I out-fail everyone here. We report on how many experiments we've done every seven days, as to innovate we have to be out-experimenting everybody. We celebrate that the experiment happens, not when it goes well.' – Steven Bartlett (Sep 2022).

'There is no failure in sports. Every year you work towards a goal. It's not a failure; it's steps towards success. Some days it's your turn; some days it's not. You don't always win; some days other people win. You come back next year and try to be better, build new habits and play better.' – Giannis Antetokounmpo, NBA player (NBA Europe 2023).

These insights from high achievers highlight a critical aspect of developing a high-performance mindset: embracing and learning from failure. High performers understand that not all failures are detrimental. In fact, as discussed by Amy Edmondson, author and professor of leadership at Harvard Business School, differentiating between various types of failure is essential. Simple failures, where mistakes are made due to negligence, offer limited learning opportunities and should be minimised. Complex failures, resulting from unforeseen interactions and circumstances, can be more instructive. However, the most valuable are intelligent failures: the unexpected outcomes of innovation and experimentation. These should be celebrated and analysed for insights (Edmondson 2018).

A personal experience of mine highlights societal discomfort with failure. After sharing a work-related failure and the lessons I learned from it, I was surprised by how many people rushed to assure me I hadn't really failed. This well-intentioned response revealed a deeper issue: our culture often treats failure as a taboo, something to be hidden rather than embraced. This fear of public failure inhibits risk taking and engagement in challenging tasks, the very activities essential for growth and improvement. In fact, considering the likelihood of failure involved in the pursuit of high performance, we're left with the challenge that if we can't find areas where we've failed, we're on a path to mediocrity.

As we navigate through failure, it's crucial we don't internalise it, remembering it's something we do, not something we are. A common challenge many face in this regard is imposter syndrome, a phenomenon believed to affect approximately 70 per cent of people. Traditionally viewed as a negative, causing self-doubt and anxiety, recent research suggests that these feelings, when managed properly, can actually serve as effective checks against arrogance and overconfidence. They can also motivate us to work harder and foster better collaboration. The key lies in balancing these feelings with a strong sense of self-worth, which allows us to maintain a healthy relationship with failure and use our experiences, including setbacks, as catalysts for growth and improvement (Young 2011; Tewfik 2022).

Principle 4: Mastering feedback

The art of giving and receiving feedback is a cornerstone of high performance. Kim Scott, the founder of Radical Candor, shared a compelling story about an employee, Bob, who was underperforming. Because of her fondness for Bob, she delayed providing honest feedback, ultimately leading to a situation where firing him was unavoidable. When she finally did let him go, Bob's poignant question, 'Why didn't you tell me sooner?', underscores a common challenge: our reluctance to deliver honest feedback to avoid discomfort or hurting feelings (Scott 2019).

This reluctance often leads to what Scott (2019) describes in her Radical Candor feedback framework as 'ruinous empathy', caring too much personally without being willing to challenge directly. However, the framework suggests that, to be effective, feedback requires both caring personally and challenging directly. Showing genuine care and belief in the person's potential significantly influences the way feedback is received. Even a simple affirmation of high expectations can dramatically increase someone's receptiveness to constructive criticism (Humphrey & Hughes Dec 2022).

However, delivering feedback effectively goes beyond just what we say. It's also about how we say it. Clarity is kindness, and being direct and honest is more beneficial than sugar-coating feedback. The common 'feedback sandwich' method, praise followed by criticism and ending with praise, is counterproductive, as it often leads to confusion or diminished impact of the feedback. An insightful example of the pitfalls of this method comes from a leadership training session I delivered.

One participant, Dave, shared a personal experience that vividly illustrates the method's unintended consequences. A senior leader who'd worked with Dave's late father presented him with a prestigious award. In his remarks, the leader included a mix of praise and criticism. He said how Dave's father would've been proud of his achievement, but unfortunately the way the rest of the feedback was delivered overshadowed the praise. Dave confessed that whenever he looked at the award, instead of feeling proud, he was haunted by the criticism embedded in the leader's remarks. This story poignantly demonstrates how the 'feedback sandwich' can lead to mixed messages, diluting the positive aspects of feedback and leaving a lasting negative impression.

While giving feedback is important, receiving it well is equally important for high performance. Effective feedback receivers manage their emotional responses, which can be triggered by the perceived truthfulness of the feedback, its impact on our identity or our relationship with the feedback giver (Heen & Stone 2014). Building a challenge network, a group of trusted individuals committed to honest and constructive feedback, is invaluable (Grant Mar 2018). The goal when receiving feedback isn't to defend or justify but to listen, understand and learn.

In summary, mastering the art of both giving and receiving feedback is essential for anyone seeking to achieve high performance. It's about cultivating a culture of open, honest communication where feedback is viewed as a tool for growth and improvement.

Principle 5: Develop good habits

The maxim 'what takes place in the shadows reveals itself in the light' is reflected in the lives of countless high performers. It encapsulates the idea that consistent habits, practised away from the spotlight, are what truly differentiates the best from the rest. Embracing 'world-class basics' means committing to excellence even in routine tasks, whether in the office, at home or on the sports field (Humphrey & Hughes 2023). Ultimately, it's about recognising the greatest threat to success is not failure but boredom, and we need to persevere, doing the things we love to do on the days we don't feel like doing them (Clear 2018).

The key to becoming a high performer lies in habit formation, transcending mere goal setting. Successful habit development is less about changing specific behaviours and more about changing your identity. For example, instead of just trying to be more organised, you should aim to become an organised person, viewing each step you take as a step towards the person you aspire to be. This mindset helps us understand that a single misstep isn't disastrous, but consistently moving in the wrong direction can lead to a fundamental change in who you are.

The lives of high performers reveal that they don't necessarily possess extraordinary self-control; they simply follow the two-step process of habit formation: deciding who they want to be and proving it with small, consistent actions. They consistently apply the four laws of behaviour change outlined by James Clear, author of *Atomic Habits* (2018), making their desired behaviours obvious, attractive, easy and satisfying. The good news is that we can all apply these laws across the four stages of habit formation: cue, craving, response and reward. For example, if the goal is to eat healthily, removing unhealthy snacks eliminates the cue, and making it more challenging to access such snacks reduces the likelihood of indulging in them.

Implementation intentions are a powerful tool for habit formation across many situations, including voting and positive health behaviours (Nickerson & Rogers 2010; Milkman et al 2011; Gollwitzer & Oettingen 1998). This involves creating specific plans for certain situations, such as 'When I get home from work, I will go for a run' (Gollwitzer 1999). This strategy can be enhanced by making the desired behaviour both obvious and easy, such as setting out your running gear in advance. You can shape your environment to make desirable behaviours more attractive and rewarding, such as finding great recipes for healthy meals or creating a positive space to exercise in. You can also make undesirable behaviours more unsatisfying, which is the principle at play with swear jars. Working with an accountability partner can also be effective in keeping commitments.

In summary, while developing new habits might seem daunting, it can be simplified into planning and creating an environment that enables good behaviours and discourages bad behaviours. It's about making small but meaningful changes consistently over time (Clear 2018).

Principle 6: Finding harmony

True high performance isn't about sacrificing your happiness or wellbeing to 'embrace the struggle'; it's about excelling while maintaining your integrity and what's important to you (Humphrey & Hughes Jul 2021). The World Health Organization (2006) defines health as a state of complete physical, mental and social wellbeing. Achieving high performance, therefore, involves finding harmony among these aspects to prevent burnout. Stephen Covey's concept of 'sharpening the saw' emphasises the importance of rest and recovery in maintaining a high-performance lifestyle (Covey 2020). Remember, the way we recharge varies from person to person, so it's vital to find what rejuvenates you individually.

Beyond rest, addressing burnout – characterised by emotional exhaustion that hampers functioning – sometimes requires more than just reducing work hours or balancing your workload. It involves finding deeper meaning in your work and feeling in control of your outcomes, elements that have been shown to be significant burnout buffers. Engaging in activities that help others, for example, can significantly mitigate burnout, providing a sense of purpose and fulfilment, even if more work is involved. Organisationally, combating burnout can also be achieved by reducing job demands, increasing autonomy and offering more support, as discussed in the 'Burnout is everyone's problem' episode of Adam Grant's *WorkLife* podcast (Grant Mar 2020).

Another element of achieving harmony is managing your

relationship with technology, particularly smartphones. The benefits of unplugging are numerous, including better sleep, improved wellbeing and reduced stress. A simple practice such as turning off your phone an hour before bed can have a significant impact. My wife and I turn off our phones on Sunday afternoons, a small act that has brought a surprising amount of relaxation and positively influences our start to the week.

In summary, finding harmony as a high performer means striking a balance between striving for excellence and taking care of your wellbeing. It's about being mindful of how you rest, finding meaning in your work and managing your engagement with technology to maintain a healthy, fulfilling lifestyle.

Application
Turning principles into practice

Grit: measuring and developing it

To assess your level of grit, consider Angela Duckworth's 'grit scale', available in her book *Grit* (2016) or on her website angeladuckworth.com/grit-scale. Remember, honesty is key in these self-assessments. For a well-rounded view, you might also seek opinions from those close to you.

Developing your grit involves nurturing your passion (see Chapter 1) and perseverance (covered in the habits section). For children, encourage grit by praising effort and process rather than outcomes or inherent talent, fostering a mindset of hard work over reliance on natural ability.

Play to your strengths

Contrary to common belief, the greatest growth lies in developing strengths rather than addressing weaknesses. In this context, strengths aren't just things you're good at, but activities that energise rather than drain you, drawing you in and causing you to lose track of time (Buckingham & Clifton 2004).

To identify your strengths, ask yourself the following questions:

+ Which activities come naturally to you?
+ Which activities leave you feeling energised?
+ Which activities do you consistently get positive feedback on?
+ When do you lose track of time?
+ When have you been successful in the past? Which skills or attributes were you using?
+ What do you enjoy learning about?
+ What do people come to you for help with?

+ Which activities make you feel you are being true to yourself?
+ If a colleague were to praise you in your absence, what do you think they would say?

Alternatively, the CliftonStrengths assessment, found on the Gallup website, offers a formal approach to discovering your strengths profile based on their research.

Manage your weaknesses

Remember, achieving high performance isn't about ignoring your weaknesses but finding a way to manage them. Consider what kind of support system you might need. Often, technology provides the solution: for instance, artificial intelligence tools can be invaluable in overcoming challenges such as disorganisation. Alternatively, partnering with someone whose strengths complement yours can be highly effective. A classic example of this is Walt and Roy Disney, who combined visionary creativity with operational efficiency to build an entertainment empire. This approach acknowledges that while you can't excel at everything, you can achieve a well-rounded, high-performing team by leveraging each individual's unique strengths.

Embracing failure

To embrace failure, first remove its stigma. Recognise that failure is an action, not an identity, and encourage open discussion about it. Seek to stay in the realm of 'intelligent failures': those that come from innovation and experimentation. Reflect on your own failures, learn from them and share these experiences. Cultivating a psychologically safe environment is crucial for this, a topic I delve into in Chapter 10. Consider setting up a failure club, where individuals can meet to discuss where they've failed and what can be learned from it.

Delivering feedback

The Radical Candor framework developed by Kim Scott is a valuable resource for mastering feedback. Aim for radical candour, caring personally while challenging directly, and avoid its counterproductive counterparts – obnoxious aggression, ruinous empathy and manipulative insincerity (Scott 2019). Brené Brown's Engaged Feedback Checklist, found on the Dare to Lead hub, is another helpful tool.

When giving feedback, it's beneficial to start by clarifying your intention to help. This sets a constructive tone for the conversation. Equally important is ensuring that the recipient is in the right frame of mind to receive the feedback.

Before delivering feedback, especially if it's potentially sensitive or negative, check that the recipient is ready to engage with it. For example, if you need to inform someone they were unsuccessful following a job interview, consider offering to schedule a separate time to discuss feedback. This approach is more considerate, as it allows the person time to process their initial emotions. It's essential to remember that the best approach for you might not be the best for someone else, so ask and don't assume.

Timely, situation-specific feedback is most effective when it's focused on observed behaviours and their impacts. The Center for Creative Leadership's SBI™ model provides a simple yet effective structure for this.

+ **Situation**: Begin by clearly and specifically setting the context. This helps the recipient understand the exact circumstances you're referring to.
+ **Behaviour:** Focus on the specific behaviour you observed. It's important to address actions rather than make it about the person's character or personality.
+ **Impact:** Explain the effects of the behaviour. This could include its impact on you, the team or the wider organisation.

For example:

+ **Situation:** During Monday morning's project meeting...
+ **Behaviour:** ...your comment about being surprised you weren't originally invited to the meeting...
+ **Impact:** ...created a negative atmosphere in the room and suggested we weren't aligned with the rest of the team.

The Center for Creative Leadership also suggests adding a second 'I', which stands for 'Intent' and encourages a discussion about why the person behaved as they did. Depending on your relationship with the person, it may also be appropriate to have a conversation about next steps to address the behaviour.

Getting feedback

Mastering feedback is also about how you solicit, receive and utilise it. Managing your reaction to feedback, particularly when it triggers feelings about truth, relationships or identity, is essential for personal growth (Scott 2019).

→ **Know your tendencies**: Reflect on how you typically react to feedback. Do you get defensive about the facts or the giver? Do you feel upset or insecure? Recognising these tendencies helps in managing your responses and focusing on what can be learned.

→ **Have a 'go-to' question:** Prepare open-ended questions that encourage detailed feedback. For instance, 'How can I better support you?' or 'What could I do to make working with me easier?' Adjust your question to suit your context and relationship.

→ **Embrace discomfort:** There will almost definitely be silence. Don't rush to fill it. If the person is struggling, ask them to think about it and come back to you.

→ **Listen to understand:** If the feedback surprises you, seek to understand rather than reject it. Asking 'Can you tell me more about that?' helps clarify the issue and shows you're open to discussion.

→ **Separate 'who' from 'what':** If the feedback comes from someone you have a complicated relationship with, try to focus on the message rather than the messenger. Extract the useful parts of the feedback, even if the delivery was flawed.

→ **Action and follow-up:** If the feedback resonates, take steps to address it. It can be beneficial to check back with the person who provided the feedback after some time to discuss your improvements and ongoing areas for growth.

→ **Make feedback the norm:** Encourage regular, constructive feedback within your team or circle. Normalise it as part of your collective growth, not as an exception or punishment.

→ **Build a challenge network:** Identify key individuals, such as mentors, peers, friends or family members, who will provide honest and constructive feedback. Ensure this network is diverse and based on mutual respect, facilitating open dialogue and regular check-ins. Use this group to validate and sift through feedback, helping you focus on the most actionable insights for continuous growth.

Developing good habits

There's a wealth of resources to help with developing good habits on James Clear's Atomic Habits website, including chapters on applying the laws of behaviour change in business and in parenting. One thing I highly recommend is to compile a habits scorecard, a template for which is available on the website, which is a way of becoming more self-aware by making a list of your current daily habits. You then rate whether a habit is good, bad or neutral based on whether it's helping you become the person you want to be or not.

There are then a few key things you can do to develop good habits:

- ✦ Use implementation intentions: when 'x' happens, I will do 'y'.
- ✦ Design your environment: think about how you can make your desired behaviour obvious, attractive, easy and satisfying and your undesired behaviours invisible, unattractive, difficult and unsatisfying.

For instance, when I wanted to lose weight, I set out with this intention: when it's lunchtime, I will work out.

I then designed my environment, opting to purchase a treadmill and put it in the garage as a cheaper alternative to a gym membership. I knew I'd be more likely to use it and, over time, I set about making the garage a more pleasant workout environment.

A crucial takeaway is the significance of consistency: avoid missing two consecutive days of your new habit. The days you push through despite reluctance are often the most impactful in cementing a high-performance lifestyle.

Key takeaways

→ By developing the right mindset, high performance is achievable for everyone.

→ A high-performance mindset is founded on playing to your strengths and cultivating grit.

→ To become a high performer, you need to embrace failure and master feedback, operating with radical candour.

→ To develop good habits, decide who you want to be and then make good choices aligned with this identity.

→ Find harmony between your pursuit of excellence and maintaining your health, remembering finding meaning in your work is a powerful 'burnout buffer'.

Go deeper

→ *High Performance*, Jake Humphrey and Damian Hughes

→ *Bounce*, Matthew Syed

→ *Grit*, Angela Duckworth

→ *Atomic Habits*, James Clear

→ *Radical Candor*, Kim Scott

→ *The 7 Habits of Highly Effective People*, Stephen Covey

→ *The Diary of a CEO*, Steven Bartlett

→ Matthew Syed, *The High Performance Podcast*

Meaningful connections

Chapter 7
Embrace inclusivity

Be inclusive by striving for both demographic and cognitive diversity, welcoming all characteristics and valuing diverse perspectives, celebrating differences, pursuing equity over equality and learning to disagree without being disagreeable.

The case for inclusion: confronting hard truths

Inclusion is a fundamental principle that goes beyond diversity, encompassing respect, acceptance and a commitment to ensuring everyone feels valued. To truly understand the importance of inclusion, we must confront some uncomfortable realities. The following section will discuss sensitive and potentially distressing topics, including rape and racism, which illustrate the profound need for inclusive practices.

In October 2017, a bombshell dropped in the form of a *New York Times* investigative report, unmasking allegations of sexual harassment against Harvey Weinstein, a towering figure in Hollywood. Hot on its heels, the *New Yorker* unleashed an even more damaging exposé, this time levelling charges of not just harassment but also sexual assault and rape against Weinstein. The alleged incidents followed an unsettling pattern: Weinstein lured women into hotel rooms or offices under the guise of professional meetings, only to make aggressive sexual advances. Leveraging his immense power, it was said he manipulated, exploited and silenced his victims.

These revelations sparked a global outcry, leading to Weinstein being convicted in 2020 of rape and sexual assault, which carried a 23-year prison sentence, which he continues to fight. But there was a bigger story unfolding. Just after the initial news broke, actress Alyssa Milano took to Twitter with a simple yet profoundly impactful message: 'If you've been sexually harassed or assaulted, write "me too" as a reply to this tweet.' Her tweet went viral, and thousands from around the world began to share their own harrowing experiences using the hashtag #MeToo, reigniting the conversation started by Tamara Burke in 2006 (Milano 2017). What started as investigative journalism morphed into a global movement, giving voice to countless victims and challenging the systemic abuse of power.

The narrative of social justice took another turn on the 25 May 2020, in Minneapolis, Minnesota, when a routine police call escalated into a global catalyst for justice and change: the death of George Floyd. A shop employee had suspected Floyd, a 46-year-old Black man, of using a fake $20 bill, and summoned the police. Though Floyd offered no resistance during the arrest, he fell to the ground as officers attempted to seat him in their vehicle. It was at this point that Derek Chauvin, a white officer with 19 years on the force, positioned his knee on Floyd's neck. Already handcuffed and face down on the pavement, Floyd gasped that he couldn't breathe. Bystanders also cried out in alarm, urging Chauvin to stop. Yet Chauvin kept his knee in place for more than nine agonising minutes, even after Floyd had passed out. By the time medical help arrived, Floyd had no pulse and was later pronounced dead. (Chauvin was eventually convicted of murder.)

While such harrowing stories illustrate the extremes, everyday instances are all too common. Take, for example, the racial abuse faced by Marcus Rashford, Bukayo Saka and

Jadon Sancho following their missed penalties in the Euro 2020 final, or the 'Surviving in Scrubs' campaign highlighting the alarming frequency with which female medical staff experience sexual harassment. Most recently, sexual abuse surfaced during the 2023 Women's World Cup, when an achievement of a lifetime for the Spanish team was overshadowed by the behaviour of the then FA president, Luis Rubiales, during the post-match celebrations.

The moral obligation to put an end to such discrimination should be reason enough to act; justice and human dignity demand it. Yet if the ethical argument alone isn't compelling enough, there's also a robust business case for fostering diversity. Cognitively diverse teams, and by extension organisations, consistently outperform their less diverse counterparts (Syed 2019). In other words, teams that can leverage diverse perspectives, insights, experiences and thinking styles create a collective intelligence far greater and achieve far more than teams that think the same.

So, whether motivated by ethical considerations, the bottom line or both, the conclusion is the same: tackling discrimination isn't just the right thing to do; it's the smart thing to do. As society grapples with increasingly complex issues, cultivating a diverse collective intelligence becomes not just a moral duty but a crucial competitive advantage.

Bias, prejudice and discrimination

There are three main barriers to inclusivity, both in the workplace and daily life: bias, prejudice and discrimination. These barriers exist on a sliding scale, escalating in both the level of intent and the damage they cause. Think of bias as an unconscious preference, prejudice as a conscious judgement and discrimination as an action based on either bias or prejudice. As described by Kim Scott in *Just Work* (2021) bias is 'not meaning it', prejudice is 'meaning it' and discrimination is 'being mean'.

121

One striking example of how prejudice and discrimination manifest comes from orchestra auditions in the 1970s, a time when female musicians were being discriminated against, constituting less than five per cent of players in the top five symphony orchestras. Many music directors publicly stated their prejudiced belief that female players were less musically talented. The turning point came with the introduction of 'hidden auditions', conducted behind a screen to mask the candidate's gender. This simple yet revolutionary change led to women being 50 per cent more likely to progress through the initial rounds. Most importantly, it significantly increased their likelihood of being selected for the orchestra, directly challenging and beginning to dismantle the prejudiced beliefs that held them back (Goldin & Rouse 1997). This example not only highlights the insidious nature of prejudice and discrimination but also demonstrates the potential for systemic changes to foster equity and fairness.

Often referred to as unconscious, our biases reflect personal preferences we don't consciously consider. All of us harbour biases, often unknowingly, and, while this doesn't make us bad people, the real issue arises when we fail to acknowledge our biases and the harm they cause, particularly how they evolve into prejudice and discrimination. John Amaechi, psychologist and former professional basketball player, argues that unconscious bias is more accurately described as an 'entrenched assumption', emphasising that we can challenge and disrupt our thoughts before they affect our behaviour (Amaechi 2021).

One prevalent bias around diversity concerns privilege. Privilege is often misunderstood; it isn't about leading a rich, easy life, but rather the absence of a specific disadvantage. Consequently, many people are unaware of their own privilege. For example, white individuals may not consider the challenges they're avoiding by not having a different skin colour. Men may not think about the struggles associated with being female; those who aren't disabled likely overlook the challenges experienced by those who are (Amaechi 2021). Considered this way, rather than something reserved for an entitled few, privilege is an example of perspective ignorance, a commonplace failure to recognise our own areas of oversight (Syed 2019). It's important to remember that you aren't required to feel guilty for any such privilege; you just need to remember it's there, that it provides opportunities not available to everyone, and to take the time to understand the challenges faced by other people.

Recognising our biases is the first step in preventing them from morphing into prejudices or discriminatory actions. It's not inherently wrong to initially assume a doctor might be male or a nurse female, but it becomes an issue when these assumptions impact our judgements or decisions. In the workplace, this can be subtle yet significant. For instance, research shows that resumés with names perceived as white receive more callbacks, even if the qualifications are identical (Bertrand & Mullainathan 2003). This is often not a deliberate choice but an unconscious bias in action, and being vigilant against such biases is key to creating a fair and inclusive environment. By acknowledging and challenging your own biases, you can take crucial steps towards inclusivity. It's about being aware, staying informed and constantly striving to create an equitable space for everyone.

Cognitive diversity

Organisational failures, such as the missed warning signs preceding the 9/11 terrorist attacks, often arise from a lack of different perspectives rather than individual errors. Teams that lack this cognitive diversity, referred to as being homogenous and therefore with similar mindsets, may overlook critical information, leading to confident yet flawed conclusions, missed outlooks and collective ignorance. In contrast, cognitively diverse teams bring varied points of view, enhancing collective intelligence and a more complete picture (Syed 2019).

The danger of a homogenous team is compounded by groupthink, where the desire for harmony within the team supersedes the need for constructive challenge, undermining effective decision making. Frequently resulting from low psychological safety, groupthink can even undermine diverse teams. When an environment doesn't allow for the open sharing of diverse perspectives, valuable insights may be overlooked, thereby diminishing the advantages of team diversity.

To maximise collective intelligence, it's vital to understand how to achieve cognitive diversity and how this differs from demographic diversity. Two individuals are demographically diverse if they differ in terms of race, sex, gender or age. However, if they both attended the same educational institutions and learned from the same teachers, they're likely to be cognitively similar. Conversely, two individuals of the same race, sex, gender and age can be cognitively diverse if their educational or professional backgrounds differ significantly. When considering cognitive diversity, the salient point is that no one cultural perspective is better or worse, just incomplete, and that by combining perspectives we can build a holistic view. For instance, when asked to describe images, individuals from more collectivist cultures often focus on contextual elements and the relationship between them, whereas individuals from more individualistic cultures pay more attention to the objects and categorising them (Nisbett & Masuda 2003; Chua et al 2005). While cognitive diversity should be pursued, it needs to be relevant to the problem at hand and shouldn't be sought merely for its own sake.

The significance of cognitive diversity serves as a cautionary note to recruiting managers who look for 'team fit' during the hiring process. This practice reflects the tendency to hire individuals who resemble the recruiter in appearance and thought, often focusing on commonalities in extracurricular activities that are irrelevant to the job (Syed

2019; Grant Apr 2020). Such an approach risks rejecting diversity of background and thought, thereby forfeiting the associated benefits. Instead, recruiters should think in terms of 'cultural contribution', considering what's missing from the existing culture and what a new hire could bring to the table (Rodriguez 2015). While it's entirely appropriate to seek candidates who align with the core values and purpose of the organisation, and this approach is encouraged, hiring someone because their face fits jeopardises both performance and progress.

Finally, it's important to note the research highlighting the peril of the 'tyranny of average'. Often, systems and products are designed for the average person, which can result in catastrophic outcomes. Matthew Syed expands on this in *Rebel Ideas* (2019), illustrating how designs optimised for the average person, from aircraft cockpits to body armour and piano keys, can result in inefficiencies and even fatalities, as well as observing that there's no one optimal diet for everyone.

In conclusion, cognitive diversity isn't just a desirable trait in teams and organisations; it's a necessity for effective decision making, innovation and avoiding costly errors. It's about harnessing a rich tapestry of perspectives to navigate complex challenges more effectively.

Being inclusive

In our quest to build an inclusive society, where justice prevails and collective intelligence flourishes, our goal is clear: to cultivate an environment where everyone feels they belong and individuality is respected. True inclusivity transcends mere non-discrimination. It requires active participation: being anti-racist, anti-sexist and allies to all marginalised groups. The difference is significant. While a non-racist might not engage in discriminatory acts, an anti-racist actively confronts and challenges these behaviours, advocating for a culture where discrimination is unacceptable. Saying nothing in support of those being discriminated against makes us complicit in that discrimination.

Effective allyship hinges on three principles. First, it's driven by a genuine desire to foster inclusion, not a wish to appear virtuous. It's about addressing and empathising with those affected. Second, it involves engaging in respectful dialogue, focusing on constructive conversations and learning rather than shaming, which is counterproductive. Last, accept that mistakes are part of the learning process. As poet and civil rights activist Maya Angelou wisely advised, 'Do the best you can until you know better. Then, when you know better, do better.'

A common misconception is that inclusivity is best achieved by treating everyone the same. However, Volkswagen's #NotWomensFootball campaign, which aimed to challenge gender bias by encouraging people to view the sport simply as football rather than distinguishing it as women's football, serves as a cautionary tale. While well intentioned, this approach risked overlooking significant differences that merit recognition. For example, on 31 July 2022, a stark contrast emerged. The England Lionesses were celebrating their first major international title, a milestone for women's football, while the Manchester United men's captain was appealing court charges of bodily harm, attempted bribery and violence (BBC 2022). Moreover, neglecting to acknowledge the distinct needs of male and female athletes can have serious health implications. It may, for instance, impede essential research, such as investigating why female athletes are more prone to anterior cruciate ligament injuries, an issue significantly impacting women's sport. True inclusivity, therefore, involves celebrating differences between groups, not ignoring them. For instance, this means recognising and respecting the distinct identities of men's and women's football, rather than defaulting to the men's game as the standard form of football and viewing the women's game as requiring additional qualification.

Building on the lessons learned from well-intentioned but ultimately misguided attempts at inclusivity such as the Volkswagen campaign, it becomes clear that the goal needs to be to prioritise equity over mere equality. Inclusivity isn't about treating everyone the same; it's about ensuring everyone gets the same opportunity. It's about understanding and respecting individual needs and preferences. True inclusivity means adapting the golden rule: instead of treating others as we would want to be treated, we should treat them as they wish to be treated.

Inclusive language

One effective way to foster inclusivity is through your choice of words. Opt for clear, straightforward language over a complex vocabulary. It's not about showcasing intelligence; it's about ensuring that everyone can easily understand and engage in the conversation.

But inclusivity in communication extends beyond the words you choose. It's also about encouraging dialogue. Don't hesitate to ask questions, especially when something isn't clear. This is particularly important for leaders or influential group members. Admitting that you don't understand something can be daunting – but remember, asking questions is a sign of intelligence. It shows you're engaged and willing to learn, and it can encourage others to do the same, fostering a more open and inclusive environment.

A memorable instance that underscores this point for me was seeing Steven Bartlett being interviewed at a conference. During the session, the interviewer used a term unfamiliar to Bartlett. Instead of pretending to understand the term in order to preserve an image of expertise, Bartlett candidly admitted he didn't understand it and asked the interviewer to explain it. The effect of this admission on the audience was profound. Witnessing a figure of his stature openly acknowledge a gap in his knowledge served as a powerful catalyst for change, visibly transforming the dynamic of the session. It not only made the environment more welcoming but also significantly enhanced the level of engagement, as evidenced by the increased quantity and quality of questions from the audience afterwards.

You also need to be mindful of the impact your words may have on different marginalised groups. Language evolves, and staying updated with respectful and acceptable terminology is important. For guidance, resources such as Oxfam's *Inclusive Language Guide* can be invaluable. This guide, available at policy-practice.oxfam.org/resources/inclusive-language-guide-621487, offers insights into how to respectfully address and refer to members of marginalised communities.

Inclusive language is about simplicity, openness and respect. It's about making everyone feel seen and heard. By choosing your words thoughtfully and encouraging open dialogue, you can contribute to a more inclusive and understanding society.

Learning to disagree

Inclusivity demands that everyone acknowledges and engages with all our differences, especially when they lead to disagreements. This often means stepping into challenging conversations that many people would prefer to avoid, such as discussions on topics like politics or religion. Unfortunately, most people, myself included, have been drastically underprepared for these challenging conversations, as there's often a strong message to avoid controversial topics such as politics and religion, when we should all have been learning how to debate them respectfully. Try to overcome the pervasive mindset of 'we disagree, therefore I hate you', which impedes genuine progress. As former US president

Barack Obama wisely asked, 'How can we shake hands if we're waving our fists?'

Embracing inclusivity in your conversations means shifting your perspective. If you've been used to seeing discussions as opportunities to convert others to your way of thinking, or to what you believe is the correct way, try instead to approach them as chances to explore a multitude of viewpoints. This exploration necessitates willingly stepping into discomfort and awkwardness as a pivotal step towards opening up genuine dialogues that will enhance your understanding of diverse perspectives. Through such exchanges, all of us can learn more about each other's backgrounds and unique views. Such dialogues can also help to counteract the damaging tendency to 'other' individuals from different demographic groups, encouraging all of us to instead recognise people with different backgrounds as fellow human beings rather than as threats. This approach fosters a more empathetic, inclusive and ultimately understanding society.

Active listening is paramount in these conversations. Stephen Covey's advice to 'seek first to understand, then to be understood' highlights the importance of truly hearing others before responding (Covey 2020). Despite common advice to listen more than we speak, adults often find true listening challenging. One method that enhances this skill is the 'Rogerian argument' (named after psychologist Carl Rogers), which focuses on empathy, mutual understanding and shared common ground. The key principle of the Rogerian argument is that, instead of arguing one's own position, individuals listen and try to articulate the other position as if it were their own (Baumlin 1987). In the context of diversity and inclusion, employing this strategy doesn't legitimise prejudice; instead it aims to enable understanding of the individual's viewpoint to facilitate more meaningful conversations and change.

Investor Ray Dalio's observation that 'the greatest

tragedy of mankind comes from the inability of people to have thoughtful disagreement to find out what's true' speaks volumes about the need for productive conflict (Grant 2017). We must all learn how to disagree without being disagreeable. We must learn to focus on the validity of the argument, not the person making it, and disagree from a basis of trust, understanding each other's perspective and showing humility rather than trying to control what the other person thinks.

Furthermore, Adam Grant issues a warning for those who regularly hear the phrase 'let's agree to disagree'. He identifies this as a sign of an ineffective approach to disagreements, indicating too much persuading and not enough listening, and suggests focusing on reversing this to foster better conversations in the future. If you hear this phrase, or those like it, it's often time to heed the reminder to listen more and talk less.

In summary, inclusivity is about treating each other as human beings with curiosity, respect and authenticity. It's about building genuine relationships and embracing the richness of diverse perspectives. The call to action is clear: engage openly, listen actively and disagree constructively.

Application
Turning principles into practice

Challenging prejudice and discrimination

The journey towards inclusivity starts with self-awareness; it goes beyond passive tolerance to active anti-discrimination. Consider this a call to confront everyday biases, prejudices and behaviours that perpetuate discrimination.

Broaden your perspective: Start by tuning in to the stories and experiences of individuals from different walks of life. As explored in Chapter 8, genuine empathy is crucial. This isn't about assessing or judging someone else's experiences, but fully engaging with their realities. Let curiosity guide you; embrace the awkwardness and ask the uncomfortable questions.

Consider where you get your input from: the books you read, the people you meet, the members of your challenge network. Do they all look the same? Sound the same? Share the same background? Could you do more to spend time with people from different religions and backgrounds? Could you read books on different topics and from different perspectives?

Take the initiative: You have the power to contribute to an inclusive society. This can mean various things: voting against exclusionary laws, speaking up against discriminatory jokes or supporting initiatives such as Stonewall's Rainbow Laces. Fundamentally, be mindful of the impact of your choices, for instance whether to support events hosted in countries with oppressive laws, such as the men's 2022 Football World Cup in Qatar.

Practise inclusive thinking in your daily interactions. Take yourself outside your own preferences to consider what might be helpful for others. Adapt your communication and meeting styles to accommodate others' needs. Don't put the burden of responsibility onto other people and make them bring it up every time. Heed the warning that unless you consciously include people, you are almost certainly unconsciously excluding them (Garrod 2023). For instance, consider asking people what form of meeting works for them: a walking meeting may work better for someone with ADHD, or a different timeslot may work better for someone with caring duties. Just because you may not like a structured agenda, this may be essential for others. Inclusion means adapting to other people, not expecting them to adapt to you.

Reflect: Any effort towards inclusivity merits thoughtful reflection. Take some time to engage in reflective practice, as discussed in Chapter 4. Practising inclusivity is hard, especially when it means challenging the bias or prejudices of those close to you, and there's nothing to be gained by beating yourself up when a conversation doesn't go to plan or you fail to act. Instead, focus on doing better next time. Consider maintaining a journal to track your progress and thoughts.

Have honest conversations

Engaging in conversations about prejudice and discrimination can be challenging, but they're vital for progress. Here are tips to enhance the effectiveness of these discussions (Leslie 2022).

→ **Identify shared objectives:** Begin by finding common ground. Recognise that everyone involved likely shares a goal, resolving the issue constructively. This mutual understanding sets a positive tone for the conversation.
→ **Target the issue, not the individual:** Rather than personalising the debate, keep the focus on the issue at hand. Remember, the objective is to find a solution, not to win

an argument. Clarify the problem at the outset to avoid misunderstanding that can escalate conflicts.

➜ **Distinguish between facts and beliefs:** Opinions are often presented as facts. Differentiating between the two is essential for a productive discussion. This step helps in addressing the real issues and finding common ground. At this point, it's important to be wary of fake news and misinformation.

➜ **Cultivate intellectual humility:** Approach the conversation with an open mind. Be aware of your own biases and, if presented with compelling evidence, be willing to reconsider your stance. Demonstrating a willingness to adapt your viewpoint encourages others to do the same.

Inclusivity in the workplace

Creating an inclusive workplace extends beyond individual actions; it demands systemic changes in policies, processes and systems. Even if you're not the one designing these systems, you have a role as an ally to respectfully challenge discriminatory elements. The ultimate aim is to achieve procedural justice, meaning that even when individuals aren't happy with the outcome, they understand and can accept how the decision was made. To do this, you'll need to ensure that decisions are unbiased and transparent and consider the views of those involved (Grant 2021). The absence of diverse perspectives in these processes often leads to oversight and unasked questions, thereby emphasising the importance of incorporating diverse teams when implementing change.

Navigating workplace injustice

Kim Scott's *Just Work* serves as an excellent guide for navigating workplace injustices. Scott categorises potential responses depending on the role you occupy in any given situation: person harmed, upstander, person who caused harm or leader. Each role has its own responsibilities, tailored to solve the issue at hand, and Scott stresses these roles are not permanent identities, recognising that individuals fulfil them depending on the situation (Scott 2022).

Hiring: The hiring process presents an invaluable opportunity to shape workplace diversity. While you should hire the best candidate, ensuring you actively seek candidates from diverse backgrounds will increase your chances of doing this. You should never hire someone because of any demographic reason. Instead, focus on how you can eliminate any potential opportunities for discrimination in your processes. For instance, use redacted applications, where names and demographic data are hidden.

Additionally, seize the opportunity presented by distributed working, recognising that such arrangements further diversify your talent pools by removing geographical barriers. Distributed work also facilitates a better balance between professional responsibilities and personal commitments such as family duties, promoting greater work–life harmony. This arrangement is one of the benefits of hybrid working, which in the right context can lead to increased engagement and retention, often without sacrificing productivity and performance.

Promotion mechanisms: How does your organisation approach promotions? Is the process transparent and robust enough to minimise bias? Or does it perpetuate a 'closed network' of promotions? Often, conventional leadership profiles contain characteristics such as assertiveness and competitiveness, which typically disproportionately favour white males, despite having no impact on performance. As outlined in Chapter 6, focus on what you need leaders to do and less on who they are or what they look like.

Ask yourself:

+ Are our hiring processes free from bias?
+ Have we exhausted all avenues to attract diverse talent?
+ How about our promotion mechanisms?
+ Is our workplace culture welcoming and supportive for people from all backgrounds?
+ Do we have any mechanisms in place for anonymous reporting of discrimination?
+ Do we have any diversity in our succession plans?

Shadow boards: A growing trend among organisations is the introduction of shadow boards. Comprising a diverse group of individuals, these boards work in parallel with an organisation's board of directors, offering unique perspectives on key decisions. Not only does this method increase cognitive diversity, but it also serves as a leadership development tool and has been effective across various industries.

Preference, tradition or requirement: The preference, tradition or requirement tool developed by Ernst and Young is an effective way of improving the quality of decision making, particularly relating to inclusivity and diversity. By challenging the criteria of decisions and asking whether they're based on preference, tradition or an actual requirement, this tool helps to surface underlying assumptions and biases, and can help you to only consider valid requirements.

Consider a job advert:

+ **Preference:** Requiring a candidate to be an extrovert because they'll fit in with the team is a preference. It's essential to question whether this trait is genuinely critical for the role or if it's merely a comfort zone for the current team dynamics.
+ **Tradition:** Requiring university education is often a tradition. While education can be important, it's essential to assess whether specific degrees are necessary for the

role's actual responsibilities or if they're included out of habit.

+ **Requirement:** Stating the need for a skilled software developer is a requirement directly related to the job's core functions.

This tool can also be applied in other areas, such as policy formulation or team collaboration strategies. For instance, evaluating whether regular in-office meetings are a preference, a tradition or a genuine requirement can lead to more flexible, inclusive working practices.

Key takeaways

→ Pursuing both demographic diversity, including everyone regardless of their characteristics, and cognitive diversity, valuing diverse perspectives, isn't just morally right but essential for enhancing team performance.

→ To be genuinely inclusive, address three primary barriers: bias, where there's no intent; prejudice, where there is intent; and discrimination, where there's harmful action.

→ Being an ally is about actively promoting inclusion, addressing injustice and alleviating suffering, not virtue signalling or seeking to appear heroic.

→ It's crucial to celebrate all our differences, striving for equity rather than equality, providing everyone with the same opportunities rather than treating everyone the same.

→ Learn to disagree without being disagreeable, overcoming the divisive mindset of 'we disagree, therefore I hate you'.

Go deeper

→ *Just Work*, Kim Scott

→ *Rebel Ideas*, Matthew Syed

→ *How to Disagree*, Ian Leslie

→ 'Enchantment, with Chloe Valdary', *A Bit of Optimism* (a podcast with Simon Sinek)

→ 'How to bust bias at work', *WorkLife with Adam Grant*

→ 'Building an anti-racist workplace', *WorkLife with Adam Grant*

→ 'How to fix our polarised conversations' (with Robb Willer), *How to Be a Better Human*

→ 'How to have difficult conversations' (with David Harris), *A Bit of Optimism*

→ 'Resolving conflict' (with William Ury), *A Bit of Optimism*

→ Chimamanda Ngozi Adichie: 'The Danger of a Single Story', TED talk

→ *Conscious Inclusion*, Catherine Garrod

Chapter 8
Connecting with others

Cultivate meaningful connections by practising compassionate empathy, clarifying expectations, committing to each other, communicating effectively and creating sustaining rhythms and rituals.

Loneliness and connection

Defined as an unwanted gap in companionship, loneliness sets in when our actual social interactions fall short of our desired ones (DCMS 2018). This emotional state not only affects our mental and physical health but also our academic achievements, work performance and even brain function. The scale of the problem becomes alarming when considering that, in 2022, nearly half of adults reported feeling lonely and, in 2023, 6 per cent of adults experienced chronic loneliness (Campaign to End Loneliness 2023; DCMS 2023).

However, there's a potent remedy for loneliness: connection. At its core, connection means feeling seen and valued without judgement (Brown 2021). It's about relationships that empower us. It's embodied by the Zulu greeting of *sawubona*, which means, 'I see you, you are important to me, and I value you' (David 2017).

Three key insights regarding connection emerge from one of the most extensive studies of adult life. First, connection significantly enhances wellbeing, countering the negative effects of loneliness; second, the quality of relationships matters more than the number of them; and third, strong ties with family, friends and community safeguard both mental and physical health (Waldinger 2015). These findings provoke a critical conclusion: achieving true connection isn't just beneficial, it's essential for a healthy and fulfilling life.

Compassionate empathy

Empathy – the capacity to understand and accurately reflect another person's experiences – is the cornerstone of connection. It encompasses two primary types: cognitive or 'cold empathy', which entails recognising and understanding another's emotions; and affective or 'warm empathy', which extends to sharing and even absorbing the emotional experiences of others. Brené Brown's research underscores the importance of blending compassion with cognitive empathy to forge meaningful connections, cautioning that affective empathy can lead to overwhelm, impeding our ability to provide effective support (Brown 2021).

Complementing this, research conducted by Theresa Wiseman (1996), a nursing scholar, identifies key characteristics that define 'compassionate empathy'. This form of empathy requires you to accept someone else's perspective as their truth while setting aside your own judgements and preconceptions. Instead of trying to 'walk a mile in their shoes', an approach that often involves projecting our experiences onto theirs, you should listen to their story on its own terms. This means embracing their narrative and seeing how it resonates with your own emotions to better understand theirs. For instance, rather than comparing their experience with your own, potentially discrediting their experience with a 'that doesn't sound so bad', compassionate empathy requires you to tap into a time when you've felt a similar way to appreciate how they're feeling.

The essence of compassionate empathy lies in your ability to convey your understanding back to the other person, reaffirming what you've heard to ensure you've comprehended their feelings and validated their emotions. Practising compassionate empathy involves respecting the other person's narrative through attentive listening, insightful questions and careful clarification, all of which ensure that the individual feels genuinely heard and not alone on their journey.

Empathy killers

Just as there are guidelines for effective empathy, there are also counterproductive behaviours, 'empathy killers', that while often well intentioned, undermine your efforts to connect (Brown 2021).

Story hogging: A common mistake occurs when, hoping to relate, someone interjects with their own experiences during someone else's moment of vulnerability. While they may think this will help, it does not. Instead, it tends to derail the conversation and convey the impression that they're more interested in their own story than the person they're listening to, leading that person to feel unheard and uncared for.

For example, when my wife and I faced the heart-wrenching decision to put down our rescue dog due to safety concerns, conversations didn't become more comforting when others shared their past experiences of loss. What would've been more helpful, and indeed what was needed, was the opportunity to talk through our feelings and situations in our own words. Having others provide a listening ear without rushing to fill the space with personal anecdotes would have allowed us to process our grief more fully and feel genuinely understood. This approach emphasises the importance of personal, attentive listening over the instinct to relate through our own stories, especially in moments of profound sadness or difficulty.

Sympathy vs empathy: Another counterproductive response is sympathy – expressing pity from a safe distance. Though typically rooted in a desire to be kind, sympathy can unintentionally magnify the gap between listener and the person who's suffering. It may also come across as insincere or patronising, establishing a dynamic in which the sympathiser remains unaffected by such troubles. As much as it may feel hard not to respond to a sad situation, reflect on how often this response elicits a 'thank you' and nothing more.

Unsolicited advice: Often following closely on the heels of sympathy, unsolicited advice can inadvertently position the giver above the receiver, undermining the latter's sense of agency and autonomy. True support often lies in offering a listening ear and asking thoughtful questions that empower the individual to find their own path forward. It's about holding space for their experience and story rather than rushing to fill it with solutions.

Comparative suffering: This involves measuring someone's pain against that of others, perhaps judging it to be less severe. However, empathy isn't a finite resource, nor should it be treated as a scare commodity that requires rationing. Perspective is essential, but every act of empathetic engagement strengthens connection. It's a collective gain, not a competitive hierarchy (Brown 2021).

The 'silver lining' mentality: Attempting to find a positive spin on someone's pain often minimises their feelings, resulting in disconnection. While tempting, it's extremely rare for someone's suffering to be alleviated by an 'at least', and this phrase deserves its place on the list of banned phrases you should avoid in your pursuit of becoming a better human.

In essence, empathy requires you to navigate your own impulse to relate, fix or compare, instead focusing on truly hearing and understanding the other person. By avoiding these empathy killers, you can foster deeper, more meaningful connections.

Presence over problem solving

When people confide in you, they're often seeking empathy, not solutions. Acknowledging their distress without attempting to immediately mitigate it is the key to avoiding these empathy killers and is at the heart of compassionate empathy. This approach, prioritising presence over problem solving, is captured in the ethos of Henri Nouwen, a priest and professor, who emphasised the importance of being the friend who can sit silently with us in our moments of despair or confusion. He advocated for being able to accept not knowing and not healing, simply being with friends in moments of powerlessness (Nouwen 2004). This involves connecting through shared humanity, being present in someone's pain and tolerating the darkness without rushing to turn on the light.

For me, this principle became vividly clear years ago when a friend lost his mother and sister in quick succession. During this time, my role wasn't to offer empty consolations or to try to fill the silence with clichéd comforts. Instead, it was about being there, creating a space for him to navigate his feelings and process his grief at his own pace. This experience underscored the profound power of just being present, offering support without the pressure of finding the 'right' words.

In those dark times, aside from listening, offering help is valuable, but the manner of our offer matters greatly. Asking someone what they need can inadvertently add to their stress, making them consider the size or appropriateness of their request. Instead, adhering to the platinum rule of friendship, treating others as they wish to be treated, calls for a proactive approach, utilising our understanding of the person to offer specific and thoughtful assistance (Brown 2021). This could mean providing practical support during difficult times, such as preparing a meal, helping with childcare or cleaning the house for them. In essence, when others face adversity, it's about making it clear that you're there for them, starting with considered acts of kindness rather than attempts at problem solving.

Finally, becoming a question-asking friend is central to compassionate empathy, as opposed to the 'non-question-asking friend' who remains disengaged from others' lives (Urban 2014). The silence of friends during tough times can be confusing and upsetting, but unfortunately seeing someone go through adversity can bring out this behaviour in friends who normally do ask questions. The critical takeaway here is the ridiculousness of avoiding asking about someone's wellbeing out of concern for reminding them of their adversity – an adversity they live with constantly. Avoiding the topic doesn't spare them pain; it isolates them, signalling indifference rather than concern (Brown 2021).

The four Cs of connection

While a lot of the research on close relationships is based on romantic relationships, many of the conclusions and principles can apply to any significant bond. In romantic relationships specifically, it's essential to understand the difference between the temporary emotional high that can be experienced in the early stages, which is better defined as infatuation, and the sustaining love that evolves over time. This sustaining love – the continued choice to prioritise another person's happiness and wellbeing – is real love. This distinction is important, as it challenges a common misconception – the idea that we 'fall out of love' with someone, when in fact we choose to stop loving them. It's often little by little, often without realising it, and sometimes for very good reasons, but we do choose to stop loving them. It's important to note that while this chapter is focused on how to make relationships work, there are valid reasons to end a relationship, such as domestic abuse, and these principles must never be used to force someone to stay in an unhealthy or toxic relationship.

The concept of love has been defined in various ways, enduring through centuries – and the biblical description remains relevant today: 'Love is patient and kind. Love is not jealous or boastful or proud or rude. It does not demand its own way. It is not irritable, and it keeps no record of being wronged. It does not rejoice about injustice but rejoices whenever the truth wins out. Love never gives up, never loses faith, is always faithful, is always hopeful, and endures through every circumstance.' (New Living Translation Bible 2015) Modern interpretations, such as Brené Brown's focus on vulnerability and love being something we nurture rather than give or get, or Gary Chapman's emphasis on expending energy to benefit another person in *The Five Love Languages* (1992), offer nuanced expansions of this age-old definition.

While romantic love often appears mysterious and elusive, extensive research has dissected what makes relationships last. Dr John Gottman's research is particularly striking, predicting with more than 90 per cent accuracy which couples will last, based on a mere 15-minute observation. His seven principles offer a roadmap to relational success, emphasising the importance of deep friendship and emotional intelligence as well as understanding, honouring and respecting each other. He also points out key relationship red flags, the 'Four Horsemen': criticism, contempt, defensiveness and stonewalling. Gottman's research (1999) advocates for prevention over cure, underlining that whatever the state of your relationship, you'll benefit enormously from working on it.

Drawing on these insights, along with other significant contributions to the field of successful relationships, this chapter introduces a framework I've developed, which I've called the 'four Cs of connection': clarify, commit, communicate and create. Each 'C' represents a fundamental pillar I believe is essential for building and maintaining healthy relationships. By embracing these principles, you can pave the way for deeper and more fulfilling connections.

1. Clarify

The first 'C' of connection, clarify, focuses on making clear the expectations you bring into the relationship. This is crucial in three key areas: the expectations you have for your own life, the expectations you have of your partner and those you have for the relationship itself. Unmet expectations are often at the heart of disappointments, making it vital to get them out in the open from the outset. Discussing these expectations is not only essential for romantic relationships but also enriches your interactions in the workplace and with your family and friends, especially when determining if someone is looking for advice or simply needs to be heard. Doing this also protects against what Brené Brown terms 'stealth expectations' – expectations we have but don't discuss that cause conflict, as while surfacing an expectation doesn't guarantee its fulfilment, it does ensure a conversation and hopefully the avoidance of disappointment (Brown 2021).

Compatible couples have compatible life goals. Early in a relationship, it's vital to openly discuss these goals, as conflicting aims will cause long-term issues. Key factors to consider include whether both of you want children, as well as career ambitions, travel plans, financial goals and preferred living locations. Ultimately, recognising, respecting and supporting each other's life goals is one of the most important factors in creating and maintaining a happy, healthy relationship (Gottman & Silver 1999). For example, after much deliberation and resisting social expectations, my wife and I jointly decided against having children. This decision was rooted in our desire to prioritise our hobbies, quality time together and the relaxed nature of our current lifestyle – one we both value deeply.

Beyond life goals, it's essential for couples to clarify what they expect from each other, bearing in mind the mental models each person brings from their upbringing. Even without realising it, family dynamics and routines can shape our present-day expectations. For example, if one partner grew up in a household where their mother handled all the cooking and the other where their father did, this could create different expectations around this domestic task. Partners should also discuss their expectations for the relationship itself. While some of these may be covered in previous discussions, this is the opportunity to bring to light any deeply held beliefs about elements such as extended family dynamics, birthday celebrations and other significant events.

The final point to remember when examining the expectations you both have for the relationship is exactly that. Both of your expectations matter – not what others expect and not what society tells you should happen or what your friends are doing, but what both of you want from the relationship.

2. Commit

Once your expectations are aligned and you've established that your life goals are compatible, the next step is to commit wholeheartedly to your partner. In this context, to commit to your partner means respecting and honouring them, viewing each other as equals, treating your relationship as a genuine partnership and striving to maintain a healthy friendship. It's not about shutting out the rest of the world completely but committing to experience life together.

True commitment safeguards against the worst of Gottman's horsemen – contempt. Contempt arises when one partner sees themselves as superior to the other and is toxic to a relationship. Genuine commitment to each other means refraining from disparaging or belittling each other, particularly to others, while continually supporting, valuing and encouraging one another. Committing to each other also helps avoid another of Gottman's horsemen – criticism, which manifests as expressing negative feelings or opinions about each other's personality (Gottman & Silver 1999). Instead, happy and healthy partners give specific, constructive feedback on behaviours that can be changed, avoiding the words 'always' and 'never'.

Often, when discussing commitment, thoughts turn immediately to exclusivity, and this is recommended. However, commitment goes beyond that. In the traditional Christian wedding vows, couples promise to forsake all others, and this forsaking extends beyond remaining faithful. By making this vow, couples are committing to prioritise each other above all others. It's important to note that this doesn't mean abandoning friendships, families and passions, as a healthy balance is essential. However, it does mean not placing others above your partner or directing any contempt towards them. This can be a challenging dynamic to navigate, especially in transitioning roles from being a son/daughter to becoming a husband or wife, but it's important to recognise that by becoming a couple you're forming a new team, and this team might be the most important one in your life.

A red flag indicating issues with commitment is the emergence of jealousy or envy. While often used interchangeably, these emotions are distinct: jealousy is a cognitive response rooted in the fear of losing a relationship or an element of a relationship you already have, whereas envy is a more general desire for something that someone else has (Brown 2021). Jealousy can be experienced as anger, sadness or fear, and if you're experiencing these emotions, it's worth reflecting on what you're afraid of losing. If, however, you find yourself envying someone else's relationship rather than fixating on the other couple or individual, identify what it is you envy – whether it's the way they value their partner, the way they speak to each other, the gifts they give each other or something else. Once you've pinpointed this, strive to integrate this desirable quality into your own relationship (Humphrey & Hughes Jul 2021).

Commitment isn't just a one-off promise but an ongoing, active choice. It's about continually choosing your partner, every day, in every way.

3. Communicate

Although it's hardly breaking news that effective communication is crucial for maintaining a healthy relationship, it may surprise you to learn that couples get worse at reading each other over time, not better (Leslie 2022). Contrary to beloved fairy tales, enduring relationships are not just 'happy ever after', but instead require continual effort. Couples in happy relationships continue to grow together, learning more about each other, resisting the temptation to prioritise harmony over resolving tension or, worse, inviting another of Gottman's four horsemen – stonewalling (shutting down and refusing to engage in the conversation) into the relationship (Gottman & Silver 1999).

A powerful tool for navigating the complexities of relational communication is to use the phrase 'the story I'm telling myself', a technique explained by Brené Brown in her book *Dare to Lead* (2018). To illustrate its effectiveness, let me share a personal experience where applying this technique made all the difference.

One day, while driving with my wife, I started sharing something personal. Suddenly, she interrupted me to comment on another person's bad driving. I felt immediately sidelined, as if my thoughts and feelings were less important than a random driver we'd never see again. Rather than retreating into icy silence or firing off a sarcastic comment, I employed Brené Brown's technique.

I told my wife, 'The story I'm telling myself right now is that what I have to say doesn't matter to you.' This led to a meaningful conversation about our contrasting communication styles; she tends to vocalise her thoughts in real time due to her extroverted nature, while I usually internalise mine. This instance not only cleared up a misunderstanding but also led us to a better understanding of each other. Using this technique, we were able to navigate a sensitive moment, ultimately leading to more meaningful and transparent communication between us.

Gary Chapman, a renowned relationship counsellor, uncovered a key element to sustaining happy, healthy relationships: understanding each other's love languages. According to his work, there are five primary ways in which people express and receive love: words of affirmation, which involves verbal encouragement; quality time, which means undivided attention free from distractions; acts of service, such as helping with household chores; physical touch, a tactile form of affection that doesn't have to be sexual and can include hugs or a simple touch on the arm; and receiving gifts, where items serve as symbols of love rather than displays of materialism. Chapman states that identifying your partner's primary love language and learning to express affection in that specific way is crucial for relationship success, especially when their love language differs from your own (Chapman 1992).

Starting up, saying sorry and shutting up

One of the most important elements of effective communication is the way in which a conversation starts, as evidenced by Gottman's claim (1999) that 96 per cent of the time a conversation's outcome can be predicted by what happens in the first three minutes. If a conversation begins with what Gottman refers to as a 'harsh start-up', criticism or a sarcastic comment, the best thing you can do is to stop, take a break and try again. Otherwise, the most likely outcome is a defensive response, the third horseman, which is guaranteed to escalate the conflict, moving you further from a solution and closer to a negative outcome. While you don't need to sugarcoat every conversation starter and avoid negative feedback, try to steer clear of criticism and contempt (Gottman & Silver 1999).

Despite what you may have heard, love doesn't mean never having to say you're sorry. In fact, a key element of maintaining a healthy relationship is apologising effectively, accepting responsibility, recognising the harm done to the other person and committing to changing your behaviour. Going on to make the change is critical as, rather than never saying sorry, love means that when you apologise, you are saying the thing you're apologising for won't happen again.

Finally, the importance of active listening can't be overstated. For a healthy relationship, Gottman suggests that when your partner is in pain, everything stops and you listen. Genuine listening involves shutting up and focusing on understanding rather than waiting for your chance to speak, and asking open-ended questions instead of rushing to give advice. This type of listening also means giving your partner your undivided attention, ignoring your phone, social media and other distractions. Simply asking what your partner needs from you in any given situation is a powerful way of communicating that you're totally present, listening effectively and completely supportive.

4. Create

To give your relationship the best chance of thriving, it's crucial to be intentional about how you spend your time and energy. Specifically, creating space for time together as a couple isn't a luxury; it's an extension of your commitment to one another. Actively make it a priority, especially in today's 'always-on' culture, which thrives on busyness and distraction, conditions that are hardly beneficial for nurturing intimate relationships. A strong partnership requires a foundation built on attention and closeness. It's about consistently turning towards each other, engaging in small yet meaningful interactions that add up over time. In the long run, these small moments prove far more beneficial to the relationship than infrequent grand gestures or lavish holidays. Heed Gottman's warning that couples often neglect each other's emotional needs 'out of mindlessness, not malice'.

One couple I know created the excellent practice of spending one evening a week, one weekend a month and one week a year together exclusively as a couple. Another beneficial habit is the relationship check-in, akin to performance reviews in the workplace. When done thoughtfully these check-ins provide a golden opportunity to discuss what's going well and areas for improvement. Research shows that teams who conduct effective debriefs outperform those who don't, so why not apply this principle to your most important relationship? To be clear, I'm not advocating for a numerical rating of your partner's 'performance', but setting aside dedicated time for reflection and conversation can be invaluable.

Applying the four Cs to non-romantic relationships

While the four Cs are framed within the context of romantic relationships, the principles are applicable to all forms of relationships, including friendships, family dynamics and professional connections. Clarity is fundamental in any relationship; understanding and setting clear expectations, goals and boundaries can significantly strengthen bonds and prevent conflicts. This is true inside and outside the workplace, as clear communication about the nature and expectations of the relationship, including the frequency and amount of time spent together, is vital. In non-romantic relationships, commitment translates to a dedication to the relationship's health and growth. It means showing up, valuing the relationship, respecting the other person's time and efforts and actively contributing to the relationship's wellbeing.

Effective communication, the backbone of any relationship, is essential in all interactions. Clear, honest and open communication fosters deeper understanding and trust, helping to navigate complexities and enhance teamwork. Creating meaningful experiences is pivotal in all relationships. Whether with friends, family or colleagues, being intentional about the rhythms and routines of our shared lives is key to maintaining healthy, rewarding connections and safeguarding against loneliness.

Final thought: preparation over perfection

Cinema has given us countless memorable quotes, and the Marvel Cinematic Universe is no exception. One of the central themes of the *Guardians of the Galaxy* trilogy is the relationship between Peter Quill and Gamora, a story of two broken individuals finding solace and understanding in each other. In *Vol 3*, Gamora no longer remembers Quill or their relationship, providing a poignant moment when she probes his motives in pursuing the relationship: 'What are you so afraid of in yourself that I need to be something for you?' This question illuminates a flawed belief in romantic pursuits: the idea that we're incomplete and need another person to make us whole. This idea dovetails with the popular but problematic dating myth of finding 'the one'. Not only is this statistically improbable (just consider the chaos if one person got it wrong), but this myth can burden individuals with undue pressure to complete an impossible task: finding someone they're immediately 100 per cent compatible with. Rather than searching for the perfect person, instead aim to become a good partner for someone. The goal isn't to change yourself to meet other people's expectations, but to become your true self by embracing your passions and, in doing so, find someone to share your life with.

Application
Turning principles into practice

Empathy in action

Empathy is about making others feel seen and heard. It starts with small actions, such as genuinely listening when asking someone how they are. Thinking about expressing empathy through language also extends to how you engage with someone you know is having a tough time: for instance, simply asking 'How are you today?' rather than 'How are you?' recognises and therefore expresses empathy for what they're experiencing (Brown 2021).

Practising empathy also goes beyond simply sensing how others are feeling. A common misconception is that high emotional intelligence involves intuitively knowing others' emotions without asking them about it. However, this approach deprives the other person of the opportunity to express themselves and truly connect.

To cultivate compassionate empathy, it's important to ask and listen. It involves honouring each person's unique experience with respect and care. This means actively listening without interrupting, staying curious, validating their feelings and offering support without jumping to solutions.

Avoiding empathy blockers is crucial. Steer clear of these common responses when someone shares their struggles:

+ **Saying sorry**: Avoid statements such as 'I'm sorry', which can create distance rather than connection.
+ **Unsolicited advice or problem solving**: Jumping in with 'I can fix this' can prevent genuine understanding.
+ **Silver lining**: Phrases starting with 'at least' might seem positive but can come off as dismissive.
+ **Minimising or avoiding**: Comments such as 'it wasn't that bad' can invalidate their experience.

+ **Comparing experiences:** Saying 'that's nothing compared to...' can diminish their feelings.

For more in-depth insights into avoiding these empathy misses, I highly recommend Brené Brown's *Atlas of the Heart* (2021) and the associated online hub. They provide valuable guidance on empathising effectively and respectfully.

What to say instead

Understanding the right thing to say when someone shares a problem can be challenging. The appropriate response can vary greatly depending on the specific situation, the person involved and the nature of your relationship with them. Here are some empathetic responses you might consider:

→ 'That sounds really challenging.'
→ 'It makes sense you'd feel that way given what you've been through.'
→ 'What's most on your mind right now?'
→ 'I'm here for you.'
→ 'I'm glad you told me this.'
→ 'How are you coping with this?' (Remember, the tone is important here; this should be asked gently and with genuine concern, not as an exclamation.)
→ 'What does this situation make you think about?'

Remember, the key is to create a safe and supportive space where the person feels heard, understood and not judged. Each person and situation are unique, so paying attention to their needs and responses is vital. Sometimes what someone needs most is simply your presence and a dose of normality, such as watching a film, binge watching a series or playing a game together. Your willingness to listen and be there for them can make all the difference.

Clarify

The focus in this section is on bringing clarity to the expectations both you and your partner have for the relationship. The objective is to surface and discuss any expectations either of you may have, spoken or unspoken. The questions below will help you do this and H Norman Wright's book *101 Questions to Ask Before You Get Engaged* (2004) features many more. It's important for both parties to answer these questions honestly. Make sure you do so in an environment free from distractions and interruptions wherever possible.

Personal aspirations and values:

+ How do you define your purpose?
+ What are you passionate about?
+ What are your personal values?
+ What are some personal milestones you'd like to achieve?
+ Where do you see yourself in five, ten or twenty years?
+ What are your views on religion and spirituality?
+ Are there any social or political issues that hold particular importance to you?
+ How much personal space and 'me time' do you need?

Career and lifestyle:

+ How significant is your career to you?
+ How do you like to manage your work–life harmony?
+ How important are your hobbies to you, and how much time do you like to dedicate to them?
+ What are your ideal ways to spend weekends?
+ What's your favourite type of holiday?
+ How important is health and fitness to you?

Family dynamics:

+ Are children in your plans? If so, how many, and when?
+ What's your view on parenting styles?
+ Do you want pets? What kind?

+ How close is your relationship with your extended family?
+ What role do you see your family playing in your life as you age?
+ How frequently do you anticipate spending time with your extended family?

Domestic life:

+ Do you have any dietary preferences or restrictions?
+ What's your attitude towards cooking?
+ How did your parents divide household chores?
+ How do you envision dividing household chores and responsibilities?
+ Do you have a close circle of friends you see regularly?
+ Where would you like to live?
+ Are you open to living abroad?
+ What are your financial goals and priorities (eg spending, saving, investing)?
+ What are your thoughts on having joint financial accounts?

Commit

The objective of commitment in a relationship is to cultivate an environment where both partners feel respected and valued, establishing a genuine partnership between two equals. There are four key avenues to foster this level of commitment.

→ **Prioritise your partner**: This isn't about dropping everything and orienting your whole world around one person. However, it does mean making your relationship a top priority and ensuring others don't demean or disrespect your partner, be it friends, family or anyone else.
→ **Offer constructive feedback:** See Chapter 6 for how to do this.

➜ **Avoid contempt and criticism:** Be vigilant against the use of absolutes such as 'always' and 'never', which are toxic to a relationship.

➜ **Monitor jealousy and envy:** Should you experience either of these emotions, don't ignore or deflect them. Instead, refer to the guidance in Chapter 2 to discern their root cause and work out how to address them effectively.

Communicate

The cornerstone of any thriving relationship is effective communication. One proven method to enhance the quality of your communication is to understand your partner's love language. Numerous resources, including a quiz to identify your love language, are available on the website 5lovelanguages.com.

Complacency is a killer when it comes to relationships. To stay happy and healthy, we must keep pursuing one another with curiosity and interest, a process Dr John Gottman describes as updating our 'Love Maps'. His book *The Seven Principles for Making Marriage Work* (1999) contains a questionnaire that will help you do just that. It's worth noting that the best way to deepen your relationships is to ask insightful questions, rather than those that merely scratch the surface.

When asking questions, aim to make them:

✦ **open ended** – questions that don't allow for a yes/ no response foster more engaging conversations and provide greater insight into each other

✦ **follow on** – questions that lead on from something the other person has said are a great way of signalling that you're genuinely listening, interested and want to hear more

✦ **reflective** – questions that encourage self-reflection can reveal more about your partner's underlying thoughts, beliefs and emotions

✦ **non-invasive** – steer clear of questions beginning with 'why' as these can come across as confrontational and prompt a defensive response.

Some example questions you can use, and will benefit from revisiting regularly, are:

✦ What are you most enjoying about your life right now?
✦ If you could change one thing about your life right now, what would it be?
✦ How do you think we're doing in terms of communication?
✦ Is there anything you've been wanting to talk about but haven't found the right moment?

One final note on communication is to be careful about the medium you use. Written text can easily lead to misunderstandings in terms of tone and intent. If a conversation has the potential to be controversial or tense, make sure you do this verbally, even if this just means sending a voice note rather than typing a message. Face to face is still the best as this allows for the expression of tone and body language, both critical ingredients of effective communication.

Create

Intentionality is crucial in every aspect of our lives, including our relationships. Taking proactive steps to establish and regularly review the rhythms and rituals of our relationships can help prevent us from becoming the couple who wake up one day and realise they're simply coexisting in two separate lives. In nurturing a healthy relationship, it's imperative to give your undivided attention to your partner, setting aside distractions such as mobile phones to ensure meaningful connection, rather than sending the message that they're merely one of many competing priorities. Below, I present two central pillars for maintaining a healthy, happy relationship: rhythms and rituals.

Rhythms

The rhythms of a relationship refer to the daily interactions that keep the emotional connection between partners alive and well. One of the most important rhythms is the end-of-day chat. While many couples engage in the 'How was your day?' conversation, it often gets lost in the noise of everyday life, occurring as soon as one partner returns home, and often ends without any meaningful exchange. However, research indicates that taking time to genuinely reunite and discuss our day is one of the most important conversations you can have (Gottman & Silver 1999). Therefore, it's essential to carve out time to do this properly, truly listening to each other and allowing for a meaningful conversation.

Rituals

These are pre-planned activities or events that symbolise the commitment made between partners. Although these can differ from one relationship to another, there are two key rituals every couple should prioritise:

➔ **Date night**: Make time each week to focus solely on each other, whether it's an evening out or time at the weekend. It doesn't have to be an expensive outing; what's important is that you allocate time to be together, making this your priority. As life's busy pace takes over, this ritual is often the first thing to be sacrificed, which is detrimental to the relationship.

➔ **Relationship review:** Similar to an annual review in the workplace, set aside time once a year to assess the health of your relationship. This review doesn't have to be formal but should be an open conversation about how you both feel you're doing in maintaining a healthy relationship. For instance, this could include discussing progress or challenges in the four Cs. You could also consider the following questions:

- ✦ How connected do we feel as a couple?
- ✦ How well are we communicating?
- ✦ How well do we handle disagreements or conflict?
- ✦ Are our current rhythms and rituals working for us?
- ✦ Do you have ideas for new rituals or changes to existing ones?
- ✦ Are we prioritising each other appropriately?
- ✦ Are we happy with the level of physical affection in our relationship?
- ✦ Are there any changes coming up we should discuss?
- ✦ What goals do we have for the next year as a couple?

By setting these rhythms and rituals and revisiting them regularly, you stand a much better chance of building a relationship that not only endures but also thrives.

Key takeaways

→ Practising compassionate empathy is about understanding how someone is feeling while not feeling it for them,
asking questions and honouring their story.

→ Clarify the expectations that you and your partner are
bringing into the relationship to build a strong foundation.

→ Commit to your partner, respecting and honouring
them, viewing them as an equal, treating your relationship as a genuine partnership and striving to maintain a
healthy friendship.

→ Effective communication is at the heart of every strong relationship, and techniques such as 'the story I'm telling myself'
and the five love languages can help you sustain this.

→ Create a life together, establishing strong rhythms and
rituals that will serve as the core for an effective relationship.

Go deeper

→ *The Seven Principles for Making Marriage Work*, John
Gottman and Nan Silver

→ *101 Questions to Ask Before You Get Engaged*, H Norman
Wright

→ *The 5 Love Languages*, Gary Chapman

→ *How to Disagree*, Ian Leslie

→ 'Relationships' (with Christina Tosi and Will Guidara), *A
Bit of Optimism*

→ 'The no 1 sex expert: how to have great sex EVERY time!':
Tracey Cox, *The Diary of a CEO with Steven Bartlett*

→ *Difficult Conversations*, Bruce Patton, Douglas Stone and
Sheila Heen

→ *You're Not Listening*, Kate Murphy

→ 'The divorce expert: 86% of people who divorce remarry!
Why sex is causing divorces! If they say this, do not marry
them!': *The Diary of a CEO with Steven Bartlett*

Chapter 9
Working with others

Make the most of working with others by operating as an effective giver, fostering trust and psychological safety, contributing towards a shared purpose, set of values and behaviours, communicating effectively and operating within defined roles.

The importance of others

We're all familiar with the saying 'practice makes perfect'. Yet there are times when this doesn't seem to be the case. A study of cardiac surgeons revealed a surprising insight: a surgeon's experience improved patient outcomes only at the same hospital. In a new setting, their skills seemingly reset (Huckman & Pisano 2006). This phenomenon isn't isolated, as team cohesion often trumps individual expertise. For example, star financial analysts moving to new companies experienced a performance dip lasting years unless their team accompanied them, and tired but familiar flight crews outperformed rested but less familiar teams (Amaechi 2021).

The takeaway? Your success hinges on your relationships, especially with those with whom you regularly interact, making the management of these connections crucial. In his book *Give and Take* (2014), Adam Grant presents a critical perspective: do humans interact to extract value or provide it? He categorises people into givers, who prioritise others; takers, who prioritise themselves; and matchers, who strive for a balance. While some givers reinforce the notion that 'nice guys finish last', some excel in their fields, suggesting that effective giving is very much a nuanced art. Takers and matchers, on the other hand, typically exist in the land of mediocrity, highlighting that being an effective giver is very much the strategy to aim for.

Grant says successful givers share three attributes:

→ **Infinite success:** Successful givers embrace an infinite mindset, operating so that their winning doesn't mean someone else has to lose. They emphasise long-term wins and collaborations over short-term individual gains, sharing their success and elevating those around them. This approach fosters trust, insulating them from the common pitfalls of success such as jealousy and organisational politics.

→ **Self-care:** While successful givers are generous, they aren't martyrs. They look out for others but not at the expense of their own wellbeing. Successful givers put on their own oxygen mask before helping others.

→ **Discerning help:** Successful givers aren't pushovers. They employ 'sincerity screening' to discern genuine individuals from manipulators, not being distracted by how nice they are or appear to be, but looking for clues as to whether they're self-focused or focused on others. Successful givers also adapt their approach depending on who they work with, remembering the adage 'Fool me once, shame on you; fool me twice, shame on me.'

To foster a culture of giving, introducing concepts such as 'pay it forward' can be transformative. One such initiative, the 'reciprocity ring', developed by Wayne and Cheryl Baker, co-founders of Give and Take Inc., brings people together to voice and fulfil group requests. From career advancement to unique experiences, reciprocity rings have been responsible for fulfilling countless requests, seen on platforms such as Freecycle. A compelling reason why reciprocity rings are effective is that they establish an ethos of collective giving, reducing any hesitation or embarrassment around asking for help, as well as ensuring those not contributing find themselves on the periphery, promoting generosity even among the usual takers (Grant 2014).

What makes an effective team?

Teams are a fundamental part of human life, satisfying our deep-seated need to belong (Eastwood 2022). Various types of teams exist with differing levels of interdependence. For instance, football teams work together closely, passing the ball constantly, while only two members of a cricket team bat together at any one time. What's consistent across all teams, and therefore the defining feature, is that they're a group of individuals striving towards a shared goal. While teamwork isn't always the answer, when collaboration is required, effective teams outperform individuals, succeeding more, enhancing personal growth and improving teamwork skills (Keller & Meaney 2017). On the other hand, teamwork problems account for around 50 per cent of start-up failures and are a leading cause of safety issues in hospitals, suggesting that the secrets of building high-performing teams remain elusive. These challenges aren't only immediate; a bad experience also shapes our perspective on teamwork, harms our physical and mental wellbeing and impacts our willingness to engage in future collaborations, further compounding the issue (Tannenbaum & Salas 2023).

Significant research has shed light on the key drivers of team effectiveness: trust, constructive conflict, shared commitment, accountability and focus on results. These elements are essential for high-performing teams, and it's important to remember that their cultivation isn't just the leader's responsibility; it's a collective endeavour. In the most successful teams, every member understands their role in fostering these dynamics. This means that even when you're not in a leadership position, passing the buck isn't an option. Each of us has a crucial part to play in nurturing trust, engaging in healthy conflict, committing to shared goals, holding each other accountable and keeping an eye on the desired outcomes. By actively contributing to these core aspects, we can all be instrumental in driving our respective team's performance and success (Lencioni 2022).

Two significant factors that can undermine team effectiveness are the presence of problematic individuals and the formation of cliques. Problem team members, as highlighted by Robert Sutton's 'No Arsehole' rule and the New Zealand All Blacks' 'No Dickheads' principle, can have a toxic impact, poisoning the workplace culture and harming the team's performance (Sutton 2010; Kerr 2013). While organisations can be tempted to retain or hire an arsehole, they should remember entrepreneur Holly Tucker's advice that it's 'better to have a hole than an arsehole', recognising the damage such people do consistently far outweighs their individual performance (Humphrey & Hughes Apr 2020).

Cliques present another challenge, forming when subgroups within a team bond more closely with each other than with the team as a whole. This can lead to fractured team unity and a decrease in overall effectiveness (Eastwood 2022). It's important for leaders and team members alike to be vigilant of these dynamics and work actively towards fostering an inclusive and cohesive team environment.

Contrary to popular belief, team members don't need to like each other to be effective; they just need clear agreement on how they'll collaborate. While it's enjoyable to work with people you get on with, this can sometimes lead to groupthink, where a team mirrors each other's perspectives and prioritises group harmony over constructive discussion (Syed 2021).

While fostering a friendly atmosphere, common social activities such as after-work drinks have not been found to enhance team effectiveness. Moreover, these activities can inadvertently exclude team members with caregiver responsibilities, certain religious beliefs, or those who simply prefer not to partake, raising concerns about inclusivity. More effective are interactive experiences such as escape rooms, which offer a dual benefit, providing an enjoyable way for team members to bond while offering insights into each other's problem-solving approaches. The best activities for your team will vary based on individual preferences, but to enhance performance, aim to facilitate a deeper understanding of each team member's preferences and working style.

Building effective teams

Team capability: do we have the skills we need?

To build an effective team, the first step is to ensure you have the right people, with the right skills, in the right places. High-performing teams can achieve remarkable feats, but they can't overcome significant gaps in essential knowledge or skills (Tannenbaum & Salas 2023). As discussed in Chapter 10, aligning roles with individuals' strengths is key.

When addressing skill gaps, consider the '7 Bs of organisational talent management':

+ **Build:** develop skills within your existing team.
+ **Buy:** hire new talent with the necessary skills.
+ **Borrow:** utilise contractors/contingent workers or outsource specific tasks.
+ **Bind:** retain key people.
+ **Boost:** accelerate planned promotions.
+ **Bounce:** strategically exit team members who are no longer required.
+ **Bot:** integrate artificial intelligence where appropriate.

Also, to ensure effectiveness, be mindful of team size. As per Amazon founder Jeff Bezos's rule, an optimal team is the number that can be fed with two pizzas – typically around six people.

With the right people in the right roles, you can be confident you've built the team capability needed to perform.

Next, focus on three main themes to set the team up for success.

+ **Team beliefs:** the perceptions and attitudes team members hold about each other.
+ **Team buy-in:** a shared understanding of the team's purpose and direction.
+ **Team behaviours:** how team members interact and collaborate.

Team beliefs: what do we believe about each other?

The attitudes and perceptions each person holds about fellow team members play a pivotal role in shaping team dynamics. These beliefs, whether it's trust in each person's capabilities, how welcome each person feels or concern of perceived threats, form the individual team member's truths and influence their sense of belonging. It's important to note that while you can't control the beliefs of others, you can influence them.

A critical belief in any team is the level of trust. Patrick Lencioni, author of *The Five Dysfunctions of a Team* (2002), identifies absence of trust as the primary dysfunction in teams. Without trust, there's no sense of belonging, leading to a culture where openness and vulnerability are replaced with self-preservation and manipulation. It also creates the conditions in which team members play organisational politics, choosing their words and actions based on desired reactions rather than genuine thoughts. This shift from authenticity to impression management undermines teamwork, stifling collaboration, innovation and performance (Keller & Meaney 2017; Lencioni 2002).

To illustrate the power of trust in a team setting, consider the case of Pixar under Ed Catmull and John Lasseter, who fostered a culture in which trust and safety were paramount. Their 'Braintrust' meetings, where filmmakers presented works in progress to trusted colleagues, exemplify this.

These sessions weren't about impressing the bosses but about candid, constructive feedback. In such a trusting environment, team members felt safe to be honest and vulnerable, contributing to Pixar's success in producing ground-breaking animated films (Catmull 2014).

Team buy-in: where are we going?

Team buy-in is essential for the journey towards high performance. While a leader shapes the culture with a clear vision and priorities, true effectiveness is only achieved when each team member internalises and supports these goals. It's critical for team members to not only understand but also have the opportunity to question and contribute to the team's vision and priorities. Regular review and open dialogue about these aspects help ensure alignment with the overall objectives, overcoming another team dysfunction identified by Lencioni: inattention to results, exhibited when team members aren't focused on the collective success.

An active strategy for maintaining this focus is de-prioritisation, which means looking for opportunities to stop doing things. Teams should regularly assess their activities, phasing out projects and meetings that no longer serve the team's core purpose. This approach prevents the trap of endless to-do lists and overburdened schedules. When new tasks arise, teams should ask 'What can we stop doing?' to make room for these additions, assuming they're already working at capacity. The mindset of strategic de-prioritisation is key; it differs significantly from refusing tasks on the basis of 'it's not my job'. That kind of refusal instead undermines team spirit and collaboration.

Team behaviours: how do we work together?

In the realm of behaviours, shared values and standards dictate how team members interact and perform. Team values and standards must be meaningful to everyone, otherwise they risk being adopted by no one. They can be encapsulated in statements or phrased as questions (for instance, the successful GB Olympic hockey team adopted the question 'Would a gold medal winner do this?'), and transcend mere corporate rules. They embed themselves into the team's culture, influencing new and existing members alike.

The downfall of Southampton Football Club, who were relegated in 2023, is a testament to what happens when standards aren't kept up. Then captain James Ward-Prowse reflected at the end of the season, 'From the first day of pre-season until right now, you can tell the standards at the club have slipped. We need to go away individually and as a club and assess if we've done everything we could. I don't think we have and that is a shame.' (Beardmore 2023)

Living by these values is crucial in overcoming another of Lencioni's team dysfunctions, the avoidance of accountability. When team members don't uphold the agreed standards, it's essential to challenge them. Allowing poor behaviour or underperformance to go unchallenged quickly undermines team performance and cohesion as commitment wanes, conflict is avoided and trust is eroded. The impact of peer challenge is exemplified by Kate Richardson-Walsh, who shares how a challenge from a GB hockey squad member to use a heavier weight during a workout made her realise she'd started to coast in multiple areas, inspiring her to work harder in the build-up to the Olympics (Richardson-Walsh & Richardson-Walsh 2021).

Beyond specific team values, there are key behaviours all teams must master:

→ **Situational awareness:** Being attuned to internal dynamics and external factors impacting the team is vital (Tannenbaum & Salas 2023). Belgian shot-putter Jolien Boumkwo went viral exemplifying this in 2023 by stepping in for her injured teammate in the 100m hurdles event, securing vital points for her team.

→ **Conflict management and decision making:** Effective teams employ the 'disagree and commit' strategy. They engage in robust discussions, listen to all perspectives, decide on an action and commit to it as a unit, avoiding the 'second meeting' syndrome, where agreement is reached and discredited later.

→ **Communication:** High-performing teams prioritise quality communication. They focus on promptly sharing clear, accurate information and practise closed-loop communication to confirm understanding.

→ **Debriefs:** The best teams engage in regular reviews, reflecting on what's going well and what can be improved.

Application
Turning principles into practice

Becoming an effective giver

Adam Grant's *Give and Take* offers detailed suggestions on becoming an effective giver, including a quiz on his website to assess your giver quotient (adamgrant.net/quizzes). Here are some practical strategies to give effectively without compromising your wellbeing and effectiveness:

→ **Practise expedition behaviour:** Inspired by the National Outdoor Leadership School, this involves doing your part and then contributing a little extra. Proactively offer help by asking 'How can I support you?' rather than waiting to be asked.

→ **Schedule your giving:** To balance helping others with focusing on your work, allocate specific times for both. To mitigate the risk of this impacting your own delivery, schedule time when you're available to help others and time when you're focusing and shouldn't be disturbed.

→ **Ask for help:** Contrary to what many givers believe, asking for help is essential. It prevents burnout and strengthens relationships, as those who have benefited from your help often appreciate the opportunity to reciprocate. It also humanises the giver.

→ **Run a reciprocity ring:** This involves group sessions where individuals make requests and help each other fulfil them. Ideally done in groups of 15 to 30, it leverages the collective resources and networks of the group (Grant 2014). More information and resources for setting up such rings can be found at giveandtakeinc.com.

Building an effective team

To build a high-performing team, team members need to address three fundamental questions: 'Who are we?', 'How do we work together?' and 'What's important now?'. While it may be tempting for a team leader to answer these questions alone and present the answers to the rest of the team, involving team members in the process of answering these questions has repeatedly been shown to be just as essential as the answers themselves. Provided it's done in such a way that team members can raise questions, express doubts, listen, speak candidly and engage in constructive conversations, collaboratively working through this process will significantly help to build psychological safety.

Whether during exercises aimed at developing team effectiveness or in everyday interactions, certain key principles should be at the forefront to foster trust and psychological safety.

→ **Thank people for their views**: Express gratitude for someone's point of view, especially if it differs from yours. Encouraging diverse perspectives fosters an open and inclusive environment, while shutting down dissenting views will deter others from speaking up in the future.

→ **Practise active listening**: Make a conscious effort to listen with the intent to understand, not merely waiting for your chance to respond. Active listening enhances communication and collaboration.

→ **Watch for 'emotional leakage'**: Be mindful of what your body language and facial expressions convey about your feelings. Something as subtle as a pained expression or a roll of the eyes can stifle someone's input or an otherwise promising idea.

→ **Don't tolerate gossip or negativity**: Never allow gossip or negative comments about teammates behind their backs. While it may feel like an opportunity to bond, this behaviour fosters a distrustful environment, leaving individuals to wonder what might be said about them when they're not present.

By embracing these principles, both leaders and team members can create a more cohesive and effective team environment. The commitment to open communication, active listening, emotional intelligence and a positive culture will not only improve team performance but also contribute to more engaged and happy team members.

Team beliefs

1a. Who are we? – individually

To cultivate accurate beliefs and attitudes among team members, and thereby build trust, it's essential to go beyond superficial bonding exercises (if anyone is still doing trust falls, please stop). Instead, focus on activities that deepen the team's understanding of each other in ways that meaningfully impact collaboration. Here are some effective strategies.

→ **Utilise accredited psychometric tests**: Tools such as Strengthscope® or Insights Discovery® offer teams a common language to discuss their working styles and individual contributions. These shared insights will help team members recognise the unique value each person brings and foster mutual respect and cooperation.

→ **Share personal values**: Conducting an exercise where team members share their personal values can reveal deep insights into what motivates each individual. This exercise goes beyond surface level 'getting to know you' activities and allows team members to uncover shared values, laying the groundwork for cohesive team values. Before engaging in this activity, team members can prepare by identifying their values using exercises such as the one in Chapter 2.

➜ **Engage in reflective questions**: Working together through the following questions can be illuminating. Consider:

✦ What's the single most important contribution you make to this team?
✦ What's the one area you must improve on or eliminate for the good of the team?
✦ What's the single most important contribution each person makes to this team?
✦ What's the one area each person must improve on or eliminate for the good of the team?

By focusing on these meaningful activities, teams move beyond superficial connections, developing a deeper, more genuine understanding and trust. This approach leads to a more cohesive and effective team dynamic, enhancing both performance and satisfaction. It's not just about building trust; it's about doing so in ways that are authentic and relevant to the work at hand. For example, in one instance, implementing a personal values exercise with a team laid the foundation for open and honest conversations that had previously been avoided. This exercise allowed team members to gain insights into each other's core values and perspectives. Following this, one team member felt empowered to show vulnerability by sharing their feelings about how the team's feedback on a project was delivered. Their openness sparked a transformative discussion, leading to a significant shift in how the team communicated and collaborated.

1b. Who are we? – collectively

Having developed an understanding of each individual team member, the next step is to define a collective identity. This identity is anchored in three core pillars: purpose (or vision), values and behaviours. It's vital to involve all team members in the co-creation of these elements, ensuring everyone understands, internalises and feels part of this collective identity. New members should be inducted into these principles and their arrival can be a timely opportunity to revisit and possibly refresh your team's purpose and values.

To guide you in defining your team's purpose, values and behaviours, a process sometimes described as creating a team charter, consider the questions below. Remember, what you create must resonate with everyone and avoid corporate clichés. Most teams find these aspects are best developed in a facilitated workshop, allowing for authentic dialogue and challenge, ensuring the process is meaningful and not just a tick-box exercise. A popular approach you can adopt is that of 'appreciative inquiry', focusing on what's working well and how, as a team, you can build on that success.

Purpose

+ Why are we here?
+ What impact do we want to make?
+ How do we want to be remembered as a team?
+ What does success look like?
+ Who do we serve?
+ What context or landscape are we operating in?
+ How do we align with our organisation's overall mission?
+ What happens when we're doing well?
+ What would happen if we stopped working together?
+ What are the decisions which must be taken by us, and that others rely on us to take?

Values

+ What's important to us as a team?
+ What are our non-negotiables?
+ How do we treat each other?
+ How do we handle failures and successes?
+ What won't we tolerate?

+ What do we want to be known for?
+ What does our collective mindset need to be?
+ What does it look like when things are going well?
+ What are our individual values and how do they align with our team values?
+ How do we make decisions?

Team behaviours

The real transformative moment for a team occurs when you move beyond just defining values to clearly articulating how these values manifest in everyday behaviours. This specificity in living out values is what truly empowers them. A valuable tool for this is the Operationalising Your Values exercise found on Brené Brown's Dare to Lead Hub at brenebrown.com/hubs/dare-to-lead. This resource provides an excellent framework for determining your shared behaviours in a practical and impactful way.

To operationalise your values, consider the following steps:

➔ **Values in action:** Reflect on each value and consider what it would look like in action. Ask yourselves, 'If someone were to observe us, how would they know we're embodying this value?'
➔ **Guiding questions:** Develop guiding questions for each value. These questions should be easy to recall and apply in various situations, serving as a quick check for decision making and behaviour. For instance, if you have a value around sustainability, consider the question 'Does this decision make a positive impact on the environment?'
➔ **Team specific:** Be creative and specific. Each team is unique, so tailor your questions to reflect your specific context and goals.

How do we work together?

Once your team has established who you are as individuals and as a collective, the next step is to define how you work together. One highly effective method for doing this is to create a RACI matrix, which is commonly used in project management.

A RACI matrix breaks down roles into four categories:

→ **Responsible**: These are the 'doers' who actively work on completing tasks. There can be multiple individuals sharing responsibility.

→ **Accountable**: This is the ultimate owner, the person answerable for completion of the task. While they may delegate the hands-on work to others, they retain final accountability. A key rule for an effective team is to have only one person accountable for each task.

→ **Consulted**: These individuals provide essential input and feedback throughout the task.

→ **Informed:** They may not be directly involved but need to be kept updated.

The ideal time to create a RACI matrix is during the planning phase of a project, but it can be beneficial at any stage. Start by listing key tasks or initiatives, then assign RACI roles. Regularly revisiting this matrix ensures it remains relevant as projects and roles evolve.

Clear communication

Communication plays a pivotal role in how we work together. Closed-loop communication, where the sender confirms the message with the receiver, enhances clarity and efficiency (Tannenbaum & Salas 2013). This technique not only improves understanding but also facilitates more effective disagreement by ensuring what's heard is understood correctly and there are no misinterpretations. Additionally, being aware of biases such as the 'everybody knows' bias, assuming everyone else knows what the team does, even when you've been told they don't, also promotes better understanding. By taking the time to explain and check for comprehension, or asking thoughtful follow-up questions whether you're the expert or the learner, you can foster better communication.

Developing situational awareness

Effective teams distinguish themselves through practising situational awareness. This involves conscious monitoring of each other, team performance and the operational environment, and then adjusting their behaviour in response. Such ongoing vigilance to both internal dynamics and external factors empowers teams to address challenges and seize opportunities effectively.

To address and enhance your team's situational awareness, consider reflecting on the following questions.

Internal team dynamics:

+ How aware are we of what's happening with each team member?
+ How effectively do we look out for and help each other?
+ How do we communicate with each other?
+ How do we ensure every team member's voice is heard?
+ Do we cooperate or compete?
+ How do we celebrate success?
+ What processes do we have in place to adapt to changes?
+ How do we learn from failures and setbacks?

External monitoring and adaptation:

+ What external factors influence our work, and how do we monitor them?
+ How do we adapt to changes in our environment or industry?
+ How do we prioritise our tasks and projects?
+ What's our back-up plan?

Conducting effective debriefs

Debriefing is an essential tool for enhancing team situational awareness and other key behaviours. Teams that regularly engage in debriefs outperform others by an average of 20 per cent (Tannenbaum & Salas 2023). Here are some essential tips for conducting effective team debriefs:

➔ **Keep it short:** Get in the habit of debriefing regularly, making it a standard part of your team routine, rather than waiting for a project's conclusion.

➔ **Leaders go last:** Allow team members to speak first so the leader's perspective does not unduly influence others.

➔ **Encourage participation:** Actively encourage everyone to participate, focusing on collective improvement without criticising individuals. This approach is not only more productive but also helps to build psychological safety.

➔ **Engage the elephants:** Address the obvious yet unspoken issues. If there are ways in which people can collaborate more effectively, ensure these are discussed, even if it requires arranging a private follow-up conversation.

➔ **Identify the root cause:** Dig deeper where necessary. For example, in the context of situational awareness, establish whether team members are failing to notice that a teammate needs help, or if they're noticing but not acting. These two scenarios require vastly different solutions.

➔ **Find balance:** Strive to identify at least one success and one area for improvement in every debrief. If the focus is always on solving problems, teams may overlook what went well. Conversely, if every debrief is a celebration, teams may become complacent. Ensuring a balanced perspective will aid in continuous development and boost collective efficacy.

Team priorities: what's important now?

The final step in building an effective team is establishing clear team priorities. This involves creating a shared 'to-do' and 'to-don't' list. Addressing this last allows team members to evaluate each task or project against the team's established purpose, determining whether it contributes to that purpose. If a task or project doesn't support your purpose, you should consider whether it needs doing.

To set priorities effectively as a team, consider using well-known tools adapted for collective use:

→ **Covey's prioritisation matrix:** This tool helps to categorise tasks based on their urgency and importance (Covey 2020).

→ **MoSCoW method:** In this context you can use this method to rank tasks in terms of 'must do', 'should do', 'could do' and 'won't do' (see Chapter 5).

Team alignment

The essence of building an effective team lies in fostering a shared understanding among all its members. It's crucial for a team to be united in its purpose and aligned in its objectives to achieve success. This unity is built through a combination of understanding individual roles, efficient collaboration, adherence to team values and alignment with the team's overarching purpose.

To achieve this level of understanding and unity, consider these steps:

✦ Regularly revisit and discuss the team's purpose and values.

✦ Ensure clarity of roles and responsibilities through tools such as the RACI matrix.

✦ Encourage open communication and effective debriefs to foster situational awareness.

✦ Continuously align and realign team activities and priorities with the established purpose.

Reflect on these aspects within your team. Is everyone aligned with the purpose? Does each person understand and value each other's roles? How can your communication and collaboration be improved to achieve your goals?

By actively working on these elements, teams can create a strong foundation for success, adaptable to various settings. The key is in the collective effort, ensuring every member is not just involved but also an integral part of the team's journey towards its goals.

Key takeaways

→ Be a successful giver by adopting an infinite mindset, looking after yourself and helping others who genuinely deserve it.

→ Get the right people on the team by selecting people with the right skills and experience, avoiding arseholes and resisting the formation of cliques.

→ Invest the time in ensuring team members have accurate beliefs about each other, fostering trust and psychological safety.

→ Establish a shared understanding of the team's purpose, values and behaviours and ensure every team member buys into this and is on the same page.

→ Define everyone's roles and regularly review how well the team is working together, engaging in effective debriefs.

Go deeper

→ *Give and Take*, Adam Grant
→ *Culture Code*, Daniel Coyle
→ *Five Dysfunctions of a Team*, Patrick Lencioni
→ *Teams that Work*, Scott Tannenbaum and Eduardo Salas
→ *Belonging*, Owen Eastwood
→ *The No Asshole Rule*, Robert Sutton
→ *Winning Together*, Helen and Kate Richardson-Walsh
→ *Fearless Organisation*, Amy Edmondson
→ *The Joy of Work*, Bruce Daisley
→ 'The office without assholes', *WorkLife with Adam Grant*
→ 'The science of productive conflict', *WorkLife with Adam Grant*

Chapter 10
Leading others

Lead others well by focusing on what you need to do rather than who you need to be, creating psychologically safe environments, setting high performance standards and engaging others on a rational and emotional level.

What it means to lead

While the insights in previous chapters are applicable at any stage of your career, this chapter specifically addresses those who are currently in leadership roles or aspire to hold such positions. However, it's important to understand that the principles discussed here extend beyond traditional workplace hierarchies. Leadership can manifest in various settings, from volunteer work to personal hobbies and interests. Whether you're already guiding a team or preparing to step into a leadership role, the guidance offered in this chapter aims to enhance your effectiveness and readiness to lead.

Leaders have existed since the dawn of civilisation, paralleled by our ongoing quest to define effective leadership. The age-old debates resurface frequently. Are leaders born or made? What's the best leadership style? Do men or women make better leaders? As with most debates of this kind, the answers often boil down to 'both' and 'it depends'. Yet, one recurring theme stands out: the importance of focusing on what we want our leaders to do, not who we want them to be.

Consider how some organisations embody this principle.

One renowned company encourages its leaders to 'imagine the future, inspire the team and make it happen'. Another advocates for leaders to 'coach your team, show appreciation and lead with trust' (Adams 2021). By adopting this perspective, leadership is reframed as a skill set that can be developed rather than an innate set of characteristics. This acknowledges that while some may naturally excel at these skills, they're ultimately accessible and improvable for everyone, thereby resolving the 'born versus made' debate. The beauty of this approach lies in its flexibility, allowing you to adapt your style to fit the situation, rather than conforming to a single 'best' style. This adaptability aligns with the notion that effective leadership isn't about things like gender, but about embodying qualities such as compassion and collaboration (Mahdawi 2022).

Before exploring our expectations for leaders, it helps to understand the distinction between management and leadership, another enduring debate with a relatively straightforward answer. As Peter Drucker, considered by many to be the father of modern business management, observed, management focuses on doing things right, whereas leadership ensures we're doing the right things (Covey 2020). However, it's exceedingly rare to find someone functioning purely as a leader or manager. To achieve success, therefore, individuals need to be capable of both. Stephen Carter, CEO of Informa, encapsulates this by urging his leaders to 'keep an eye on the far' to secure a promising future, and 'deliver today' to bring that future to fruition.

Therefore, moving beyond the conventional separation of managers and leaders and based on my own research, I propose the concept of 'managerial leadership'. This term represents a role that integrates both managing and leading, which are essential for driving performance and achieving success. As you embark on your leadership journey, consider how managerial leadership might manifest in your professional development.

Intent-based leadership

As he stepped into his first command on the USS Santa Fe, then the worst-performing submarine in the US Navy, Captain Marquet faced a daunting challenge. His task was made more complex by his unfamiliarity with this particular submarine, having prepared for a different command. During a routine drill simulating a fault, Captain Marquet ordered 'ahead two thirds'. The officer on deck repeated the order, yet nothing happened. Approaching the unsettled helmsman, Captain Marquet uncovered a startling truth: unlike his previous submarines, the Santa Fe lacked a two thirds mode. Despite knowing this, the officer had still dutifully repeated the order (Marquet 2013).

Captain Marquet transformed the Santa Fe from the fleet's worst to its best by employing what he termed 'intent-based leadership'. He defined this as a leader's goal being 'to give no orders, but to provide direction and intent, allowing others to figure out the path and means to achieve it'. Simon Sinek (2014) echoes this sentiment, stating that 'leadership is not about being in charge, but taking care of those in your charge'. Research strongly supports this view, indicating that a blend of deep support and relentless challenge promotes individual and team excellence (Duckworth 2016). Integrating these ideas with Amy Edmondson's research on psychological safety (2018), I believe there are two vital components of effective managerial leadership: establishing high performance standards and creating an environment that enables people to perform.

Enable people to perform

When operating as a managerial leader, your primary role is to be an enabler, striving to uplift those around you. You'll understand that your success hinges on your followers, a recognition that sets you apart from individual performers. This naturally leads to the question 'How do I get the most from my team?' Yet this mindset can inadvertently lead to treating people as mere resources, and this will erode any healthy culture (Sinek 2014). A more human-centred approach is to ask 'How can I create an environment where individuals feel they belong and can perform at their best?'

The key lies in fostering a psychologically safe environment. In such a space, team members feel confident to share ideas, questions or concerns, free from the fear of negative repercussions to themselves, their status or their careers. It's a setting in which trust and respect flourish and candour is valued (Edmondson 2018). It's important to distinguish psychological safety from comfort. Psychological safety is about individuals feeling safe enough to be uncomfortable, challenge each other and take ownership of their impact on others (Amaechi 2021; Richardson-Walsh & Richardson-Walsh 2021). Psychological safety is also about team members feeling able to report mistakes. This transparency drives team performance as it enables mistakes to be addressed and prevented in the future (Humphrey & Hughes Dec 2022). The advantages of psychological safety, enhanced performance, innovation, engagement and resilience have been consistently demonstrated across various industries and contexts. Frequently cited as the most important factor for success, psychological safety sets teams and organisations on a path to success. Without it, internal conflicts can drain an organisation's ability to confront external challenges effectively (Duckworth 2016; Humphrey & Hughes Dec 2022; Kahn 1990; MOD 2022).

Creating a psychologically safe environment requires everyone to be authentic, transparent and consistent. Authenticity, which is discussed in relation to vulnerability in Chapter 3, becomes even more important as you assume leadership roles. Just as authenticity influences trust, the degree of transparency exhibited by a leader significantly impacts their level of trustworthiness. However, it's crucial to maintain a balance, providing enough context for decisions without oversharing every detail (Sinek 2023). Finally, consistency is vital. Unpredictable leadership breeds uncertainty, leaving followers feeling insecure and fearful, which directly undermines the foundation of a psychologically safe environment (Groeschel 2018).

Treat people as individuals

Contrary to the golden rule, great managers understand that effective leadership requires a personalised approach. Rather than treating everyone as they themselves would like to be treated, they tailor their approach to each individual's preferences. Great managers approach their role like a game of chess rather than draughts, recognising that each individual has unique strengths, needs and abilities.

To treat people as individuals, the first step is to understand their strengths and capabilities. Then you can help them to maximise their potential. This approach aligns with high-performance principles, but as a managerial leader, you have the unique opportunity to design roles around people's strengths. It's also beneficial to create partnerships that address weaknesses rather than focusing solely on developing these areas, which often leads to marginal improvements and can demotivate even the most promising team members (Buckingham 2005).

The second aspect involves understanding individual motivations. While fair compensation is essential, it's important to recognise that monetary incentives aren't strong long-term motivators. In contrast, autonomy is a significant driver of motivation as it gives individuals a sense of control over their work. This control can be shaped within Dan Pink's 'four Ts' framework (2018), giving people control over what they do (Task), how they spend their working days (Time), how they approach their work (Technique) and who they work with (Team).

Set high performance standards

It's important to remember that enabling people to perform doesn't mean relinquishing your accountability or decision-making responsibility and just allowing individuals to do as they please. This laissez-faire leadership approach, characterised by such behaviours, has been consistently found to be ineffective. Instead, exceptional managerial leaders embrace a 'tight, loose, tight' approach (Guthridge 2018). They are tight on the purpose and goals of the organisation, loose on the how of execution, providing flexibility and autonomy, and tight again on accountability for results. This accountability also extends to challenging poor performance with radical candour, as great managerial leaders recognise that the impact of not addressing under-performance far outweighs the difficulty and consequences of an awkward conversation.

This tight-loose-tight method aligns with Simon Sinek's 'Start with Why' philosophy, as it emphasises the leader's role in communicating the why while empowering individuals to determine the how and what (Sinek 2011). In dynamic army operations, commanders exemplify this approach by crafting intent statements, a broad outline of what a successful mission should achieve, enabling individuals to adapt to changing circumstances.

Defining organisational culture is arguably the most critical responsibility of a managerial leader. Beyond superficial gestures such as installing a pool table in the break room, culture is shaped by the decisions you make, the behaviours you encourage and the worst you're prepared to tolerate (Amaechi 2021). As a managerial leader, it falls upon you to shape the culture by establishing clear a vision as well as defined values and behaviours, and embodying them consistently. This includes active listening, making values-based decisions and exhibiting behaviours that reflect these values. If you fail to live by your values, you risk creating superficial slogans without the substance to effect meaningful change.

Recognising that any culture is defined by your decisions and behaviours will challenge you to envision and actively cultivate your desired culture. A remarkable example of effective cultural development can be found in the book *Winning Together* (2021) by Helen and Kate Richardson-Walsh, who discuss the impact of specific behavioural statements on the Olympic gold medal-winning GB hockey team (Richardson-Walsh & Richardson-Walsh 2021).

Navigating complexity

In addition to culture, managerial leaders play a pivotal role in setting strategy and direction. This requires adopting an outside-in perspective, understanding external factors and incorporating them into organisational strategy and priorities. Agility and the ability to navigate complexity are also vital, especially in responding to threats and opportunities while staying aligned with the organisation's purpose and values.

Despite the myriad of changes resulting from the Covid-19 pandemic, research emphasises that the fundamentals of good leadership, while unchanged, became even more significant (Corporate Research Forum 2022). The pandemic particularly necessitated for many a rapid development in leading a distributed workforce. With distributed work levels remaining higher than in pre-pandemic times, the hybrid work model has become a new norm. As a leader, you need to make sure you've adapted to this shift, considering aspects such as online presence, accessibly, authenticity, trust and fairness. It's also critical to be mindful of proximity bias, which can result in leaders favouring those who are physically closer. For instance, in a hybrid work environment where leaders may only be in the office on certain days, there's a risk of repeatedly interacting with the same people and inadvertently overlooking others. To overcome this, managerial leaders should be conscious of this bias and take deliberate actions to include and engage with all team members, regardless of physical proximity (Gartner 2020).

Effective leadership in this hybrid landscape demands adaptability and a deep understanding of the unique challenges and opportunities it presents. Leaders must navigate the balance between virtual and in-person interactions, ensuring that communication, collaboration and team cohesion are maintained across different working environments. This involves not only considering your leadership style but also rethinking how to measure performance, provide feedback and maintain team dynamics in a landscape where traditional office interactions are no longer the norm.

In summary, as a managerial leader, your role extends beyond merely setting objectives and overseeing tasks. You must foster environments that encourage high performance, ensure psychological safety and adapt to evolving work landscapes. By doing so, you can create cultures that not only drive success but also resonate with the values and aspirations of your team, ensuring sustainability and resilience in your organisation.

Leading change

The year 2000 witnessed a classic David and Goliath tale in the movie rental industry. A small, ambitious start-up equipped with a revolutionary concept approached a mighty, well-established giant dominating the market. This underdog had a vision that promised to reshape the way people enjoyed movies, offering a glimpse into the future of entertainment. Excited about the potential collaboration, the start-up finally met with the industry titan and presented an offer they believed to be irresistible. For just $50 million, they proposed integrating their innovative online movie rental service into the portfolio of the already thriving company. However, the outcome was far from what they expected. The company's representatives, barely suppressing laughter, scoffed at the idea, dismissing it as ludicrous (Randolph 2021).

Over the next decade, the movie rental industry underwent a seismic shift. The once-dominant colossus, valued at $8.4 billion, crumbled into bankruptcy, unable to adapt to the changing times. Meanwhile, the once-underestimated start-up evolved into a global juggernaut. By 2020, its value had skyrocketed to an astonishing $203 billion.

By now, you may have already guessed the identities of these legendary players. The giant that fell from grace was Blockbuster, the household name that at one point seemed to have a shop on every high street. And the triumphant underdog, rising from obscurity? It was none other than Netflix, the trailblazer that forever changed the way we consume entertainment.

The phrase 'that's the way we do things' ranks among the most dangerous in the English language, symbolising a stagnant environment resistant to improvement and innovation. When companies do attempt to implement change, it's disconcerting to note that approximately two thirds of major change initiatives fail, with up to 72 per cent of these failures attributable to internal sabotage (Keller & Meaney 2017). This suggests not only a general aversion to change but also a widespread inability to manage it.

Before exploring change management models, it's important to emphasise the criticality of communication – above all, the key action to prioritise what I call relentless communication. It's vital to communicate, communicate and then communicate again, reinforcing messages to prevent misunderstandings and negative assumptions that often arise in the absence of clear information. Failure to communicate creates a void that people will fill, often with rumours or negative assumptions that can be more damaging than even the most difficult messages you may need to convey. When contemplating change, consider the advice of Chris Voss, former lead hostage negotiator for the FBI, who suggests focusing on becoming 'people movers' rather than immediate problem solvers (Voss & Raz 2017).

In navigating the complexities of leading change, two frameworks stand out for their effectiveness: Chip and Dan Heath's concept of the rider and the elephant, and John Kotter's eight-step model. The Heath brothers' model recognises that we're influenced by two forces: emotions and logic. Emotions are depicted as a powerful elephant, driven by impulse, while logic is the rider who, though weaker, can direct the elephant when properly engaged. They advocate for engaging both the emotional (elephant) and logical (rider) aspects, communicating on both levels to facilitate change. They also highlight the need to shape the path, making it easier to adopt new behaviours (Heath & Heath 2010).

If you're seeking a more structured approach to leading change, John Kotter's eight-step model (2012) offers a comprehensive guide to increase the likelihood of success:

1. **Create a sense of urgency:** It's vital for everyone impacted by the change to understand the reasons why the change needs to happen. Despite its importance, this step is often overlooked or minimally addressed.
2. **Establish a guiding coalition:** Forming a group responsible for leading the change, often known as a steering group, is key to staying on track and managing issues as they arise.
3. **Develop a vision:** If you don't know where you're going, you can guarantee you won't get there. Therefore, when managing change, define the vision early, focusing on what the end result will look like and align it with the initial sense of urgency.
4. **Communicate the vision:** Even the strongest vision is ineffective if it's not communicated. Reiterate the vision

until it becomes second nature to everyone involved.

5. **Remove obstacles:** Change journeys inevitably encounter obstacles. Regularly assessing and addressing these challenges is essential to maintaining momentum.

6. **Celebrate small wins:** Change processes are often lengthy and challenging, frequently suffering from Kanter's law, which states that everything looks like a failure in the middle. By setting and celebrating small milestones, motivation and progress are maintained.

7. **Consolidate gains:** Analyse the small wins for further improvement opportunities. Building on progress solidifies the change and ensures its sustainability.

8. **Anchor the change:** Make the change part of the organisation's fabric by sharing success stories, celebrating significant achievements and ensuring leadership engagement.

The concept of immunity to change suggests that resistance often stems from conflicting commitments and underlying assumptions, not merely a lack of desire for change. For instance, a heart patient may simultaneously desire a healthy lifestyle and indulge in unhealthy habits. Therefore, until you understand these competing commitments and underlying assumptions, you won't be able to overcome your, or your organisation's, resistance to change and successfully implement the changes you're looking for (Keegan & Lahey 2009).

Application
Turning principles into practice

Focus on what leaders do rather than who they are

Whether you're in a leadership role or are responsible for developing leaders in your organisation, the emphasis needs to be on the actions that leaders take rather than who they need to be. This approach allows individuals to lead authentically, leveraging their unique style and strengths rather than emulating others. Operating ethically is paramount for leaders, transcending legal compliance and embodying a profound responsibility towards their teams and society. Only such ethical leadership can create high-performing organisations that people aspire to join.

One practical step in fostering this mindset is to create a personalised version of the MBA Oath, originally crafted by Harvard Business School graduates in 2009 as a 'Hippocratic Oath for Managers'. Those graduating from accredited MBA programmes can sign this oath, and I encourage you to develop a version that aligns with your own values and principles, making it a cornerstone of your leadership philosophy.

Below is the original MBA Oath for reference:

'As a business leader I recognise my role in society. My purpose is to lead people and manage resources to create value that no single individual can create alone. My decisions affect the wellbeing of individuals inside and outside my enterprise, today and tomorrow. Therefore, I promise that:

+ I will manage my enterprise with loyalty and care, and will not advance my personal interests at the expense of my enterprise or society.
+ I will understand and uphold, in letter and spirit, the

laws and contracts governing my conduct and that of my enterprise.

+ I will refrain from corruption, unfair competition or business practices harmful to society.

+ I will protect the human rights and dignity of all people affected by my enterprise, and I will oppose discrimination and exploitation.

+ I will protect the right of future generations to advance their standard of living and enjoy a healthy planet.

+ I will report the performance and risks of my enterprise accurately and honestly.

+ I will invest in developing myself and others, helping the management profession continue to advance and create sustainable and inclusive prosperity.

In exercising my professional duties according to these principles, I recognise that my behaviour must set an example of integrity, eliciting trust and esteem from those I serve. I will remain accountable to my peers and to society for my actions and for upholding these standards. This oath I make freely, and upon my honour.'

Build psychological safety

A practical tool for assessing psychological safety in your team is the Fearless Organization Scan team survey. This survey offers a comparison with global benchmark data and is accessible for a small fee at fearlessorganization.com/engage/fearless-organization-scan-team-survey.

Creating a space for genuine, authentic connections and relationship building is central to building psychological safety. This approach, combined with a culture in which people aren't penalised for reporting mistakes and intelligent failures are recognised as learning opportunities, forms the cornerstone of a psychologically safe environment. An excellent example of this is the Lego Group, which initiated 'campfire conversations' during a period of change, allowing people to reflect openly on their experiences, discuss expansions of the changes and plan future actions (Corporate Research Forum 2022).

There is no one-size-fits-all approach to creating psychological safety, but here are some general recommendations:

✦ Invest time in building relationships with your team members. More strategies on effective team building can be found in Chapter 9.

✦ Proactively create an environment where individuals feel comfortable raising issues and concerns.

✦ Show up authentically and lead by example. Practise vulnerability while maintaining appropriate boundaries – guidance contained in Chapter 3.

✦ Celebrate the reporting of mistakes and intelligent failures. This approach doesn't prevent learning from these incidents or taking steps to prevent future occurrences; it focuses on a non-punitive response to their reporting.

Understand your team members: strengths

Working with the people you lead to identify their strengths is critical. Beyond using commercial tools like the Gallup CliftonStrengths Finder and Strengthscope®, you can engage in direct conversations with your team members by asking them to reflect on the past three months:

➡ **What was your best day at work, and what made it so fulfilling?** Explore what they were doing and why they enjoyed it so much. Remember, strengths are activities that energise us, not just those we excel at. This method might reveal areas that are energising but not yet mastered, indicating potential for further development.

➡ **Conversely, what was your worst day at work during the same period, and why was it so challenging?** This question aims to uncover weaknesses. Understanding the underlying reasons for their dissatisfaction is key to this exploration. As a leader, it's your responsibility to work with the individual to find ways to manage these weaknesses.

Finally, as you consider the strengths and weaknesses of your team, ponder this third question:

→ **How can I redesign team roles to play to each member's strengths while effectively managing any weaknesses?**

This strategic approach is essential for maximising the overall performance of your team.

Understand your team members: motivations

First and foremost, take the time to understand the motivations of each team member. To facilitate this, consider engaging in the activities from Chapter 1.

While extrinsic reward can be effective for simple routine tasks, establishing a genuinely motivating environment is essential for those requiring creativity, which is increasingly common in today's work. To motivate your followers, focus on creating an environment that nurtures autonomy in Pink's key areas (2018).

+ **Task:** allow individuals autonomy over what they're doing, aligned with overall objectives.
+ **Time:** enable flexibility in work schedules, allowing individuals to decide how they spend their time.
+ **Technique:** let individuals decide how to achieve their objectives, accommodating hybrid working preferences.
+ **Team:** where possible, allow individuals to choose who they work closely with.

In situations where autonomy is limited, it becomes crucial to invest time in explaining a task's importance, linking it to the broader purpose and mission. Demonstrating empathy, especially when tasks are mundane or challenging, can significantly enhance motivation.

In addition to shaping their environment, consider how each individual prefers to receive positive feedback and praise. Some may thrive on public recognition, while others may prefer private acknowledgement or small gestures. The key thing is that you learn to speak their language.

Work tight-loose-tight

The most effective performance standards are established within the framework of 'tight-loose-tight', which can be applied in various contexts, including business strategy and performance conversations (Guthridge 2018). Below are two examples of how this can be implemented. Reflect on how you might apply this framework in your current or future situations.

Business strategy:

+ **Tight for purpose and goals:** set by the leadership, ensuring everyone aligns with the organisation's direction.
+ **Loose for execution:** grant autonomy to business units, teams and individuals in determining how to achieve these goals.
+ **Tight for results:** hold everyone accountable for delivering successful outcomes aligned with the defined goals.

Performance conversation:

+ **Tight for purpose:** clearly define the objective of the conversation, whether it's delivering feedback, reviewing performance, or setting objectives.
+ **Loose for the conversation:** be flexible and responsive, focusing on asking questions and providing coaching support.
+ **Tight for commitment:** ensure accountability for actions and agreements made during the conversations from both parties.

Applying the tight-loose-tight framework establishes clarity and direction while allowing flexibility and individual autonomy, fostering accountability and driving success.

Prepare your leader's intent

Make it a habit to communicate your leader's intent, whether for a major project or a specific task. Based on a military commander's intent, your leader's intent statement will comprise three essential elements:

+ **Purpose:** clearly articulate why a specific task is requested and how it ties into the team's or organisation's overall objectives. If the purpose is unclear, reconsider the task's necessity.
+ **Key tasks:** focus on specifying major milestones or critical 'must-haves' required for the work to be successful, without delving into granular detail.
+ **End state:** describe what the completed work will look like, keeping it simple and concise for clear understanding.

Communicating your intent not only sets clear direction but also helps in preventing unnecessary tasks. By articulating the purpose, defining key tasks and describing the desired end state, you foster a shared understanding that increases the likelihood of successful outcomes.

Leading distributed teams

In 2020, Gartner introduced the NEAR model, a framework tailored for managing distributed workers.

→ **Normalise self-direction:** Recognise that, compared to their on-site counterparts, distributed workers often prefer self-directed work. Facilitate this by working with your team to ensure they clearly understand their objectives and empower them to take control of their work. Emphasise autonomy while providing necessary guidance and support.

➔ **Enable new relationships:** Counteract the isolation often felt in distributed work by actively helping team members to build and maintain relationships. Create opportunities for virtual interactions and foster an inclusive atmosphere in team meetings.

➔ **Accentuate the positive:** Given that distributed workers often receive more corrective feedback, consciously balance this with positive reinforcement. Acknowledge achievements and progress as much as areas for improvement.

➔ **Revamp team expectations:** In distributed settings, where informal interactions are less frequent, it's essential to explicitly set and communicate team expectations. Define how each team member can effectively contribute and collaborate in this environment.

By implementing the NEAR model, you can support and manage distributed team members effectively, creating an environment that promotes self-direction, builds relationships, emphasises positive feedback and establishes clear team expectations for successful distributed work.

Leading change

Effective change leadership involves strategies for directing the rider, motivating the elephant and shaping the path, as Chip and Dan Heath describe in their book *Switch* (2010). These tactics, along with Kotter's eight steps for larger projects, provide a comprehensive approach to managing change.

➔ **Direct the rider:** engage the logical side by specifying the exact actions you want people to take, being clear about where you're headed and why it's beneficial for all involved.

➔ **Motivate the elephant:** connect with the emotional side by creating an emotional connection with the change, reducing fear by breaking the change down into manageable chunks and encouraging individuals to recognise their capacity for growth.

→ **Shape the path:** adjust the environment and context to make the desired behaviour more natural and easier to adopt, as discussed in the habit-building section of Chapter 6. This includes making actions obvious, attractive, easy and satisfying.

Appreciative enquiry

In addressing the challenge of overcoming immunity to change, whether it's personal, within a team, or organisation wide, Keegan and Lahey's framework offers a systematic approach to identify and tackle competing commitments and underlying assumptions. Their book *Overcoming Immunity to Change* (2009) is an in-depth resource on this topic. To apply this framework effectively, consider working through the following reflective questions:

✦ What's the change you're trying to achieve? Clearly define the change objective.
✦ Which behaviours are getting in the way? Identify and list specific behaviours without rationalisation, focusing purely on observation.
✦ What's driving these behaviours? Explore the underlying concerns or perceived rewards linked with these behaviours.
✦ What are the big assumptions behind these statements? Uncover and articulate the fundamental beliefs influencing these behaviours.

Maximise the effectiveness of this process by actively engaging with your challenge network for continuous feedback. This network can also provide a safe environment to test and refine your assumptions. When implementing organisational change, adapt this framework to groups or subgroups, as detailed in Keegan and Lahey's book, which provides specific guidance on facilitating this collaborative process.

Key takeaways

→ Rather than a person you are, leadership is a role that you adopt, defined by the actions you take.

→ Although management and leadership have distinct qualities, effective leaders blend both roles, demonstrating the ability to manage tasks while inspiring and guiding their teams.

→ Managerial leaders foster high performance by creating psychologically safe environments and treating people as individuals.

→ A critical aspect of managerial leadership involves setting and maintaining high performance standards and shaping organisational culture.

→ Effective change leadership involves engaging people both rationally and emotionally and actively shaping the environment to support the change.

Go deeper

→ *First, Break All the Rules*, Marcus Buckingham
→ *Drive*, Daniel Pink
→ *Turn the Ship Around*, L David Marquet
→ *Dare to Lead*, Brené Brown
→ *Promises of Giants*, John Amaechi
→ 'Is it safe to speak up at work?', *WorkLife with Adam Grant*
→ *Switch*, Chip and Dan Heath
→ *Immunity to Change*, Robert Kegan and Lisa Lahey
→ 'The 4 deadly sins of work culture', *WorkLife with Adam Grant*
→ 'How to change your workplace', *WorkLife with Adam Grant*

Conclusion

Bringing it all together

In this concluding chapter, let's revisit the core insights in each of the preceding chapters. My hope is that these key takeaways will prompt you to reflect deeply on the ideas you've explored throughout. Remember, your journey doesn't end with the last pages of this book. True transformation begins when you apply these learnings. Use the following reminders as a gauge. How well have you implemented these principles? Where might you need to focus more as you move forward? Your answers to these questions are your stepping stones to continued growth and success.

Strand 1: Meaningful foundations

Chapter 1: Living with purpose

Live your purpose by understanding how your unique passions and skills can contribute to the needs of the world and by turning these into something you can be paid for.

Reflect on your true motivations and avoid the common pitfall of solely chasing monetary success. Instead, focus on finding your ikigai. This concept represents the intersection of your passions, skills, the world's needs and potential compensation. Utilise this framework to carve out a purpose that propels you towards a positive infinite goal, rather than away from a negative one.

Chapter 2: Emotional agility and resilience

Better understand yourself and others and equip yourself to face adversity.

To enhance your emotional intelligence, start by fully recognising and embracing your emotions, using them to identify your values and responding to them in ways that are constructive and self-aware. Build resilience by challenging the three Ps: avoid seeing setbacks as permanent, pervasive or personal.

Chapter 3: Vulnerability and authenticity

Root yourself in the knowledge that you are enough and practise vulnerability by being courageous, respecting boundaries and embracing uncertainty and emotional exposure.

Build on a foundation of self-worth that acknowledges and affirms your intrinsic value. Foster self-compassion and develop shame resilience. Embrace the practice of vulnerability by choosing courage over comfort, actively shedding the suits of armour that hinder genuine connection. Cultivate a life characterised by gratitude, a respect for personal boundaries and striving for excellence, not perfection.

Strand 2: Meaningful alignment

Chapter 4: Align your actions

Achieve fulfilment by choosing how you respond in every situation and making better decisions.

Remember the significance of the stimulus–response gap and the vital role of choosing your response in each situation. Emphasise responding thoughtfully rather than reacting impulsively. Assess the stimuli you encounter and determine whether they fall within your circle of control, influence or acceptance, then respond appropriately. Focus on building your self-awareness, develop an internal locus of control and challenge any limiting beliefs that may arise.

Chapter 5: Align your decisions

Make better decisions by being aware of biases, gaining perspective, following a robust process and considering appropriate options.

Consciously balance System 1 (intuitive) and System 2 (analytical) thinking in your decision-making process, ensuring you expend mental effort appropriately. Stay vigilant about the various factors that can cloud judgement and strive to be in the right mental state for critical decisions. Actively seek diverse perspectives and consider multiple options to enhance your decision making. Engage in a thorough process: assess your goals, anticipate outcomes, weigh risks against benefits. In group settings, be mindful of hierarchical dynamics and HiPPOs, encouraging balanced contributions.

Chapter 6: Embrace high performance

Become a high performer by playing to your strengths, being gritty, embracing failure, mastering feedback and developing good habits. Engage in deliberate practice in whatever you pursue and find harmony between your pursuit of excellence and maintaining your health.

Remember, high performance hinges not on genetic predisposition but on the quality and consistency of your practice, coupled with a mindset geared towards excellence. Focus on leveraging your strengths while developing strategies to address your weaknesses. Embrace the concept of intelligent failure, viewing failure as a learning opportunity, not a personal identity. Engage in giving and receiving feedback with a balance of personal care and direct challenge. Develop beneficial habits through implementation intentions and environment design to facilitate your journey towards high performance.

Strand 3: Meaningful connections

Chapter 7: Embrace inclusivity

Be inclusive by striving for both demographic and cognitive diversity, welcoming all characteristics and valuing diverse perspectives, celebrating differences, pursuing equity over equality and learning to disagree without being disagreeable.

Acknowledge the importance of demographic and cognitive diversity, not only as a commitment to social justice but also a strategy to enhance business performance. Cultivate self-awareness to actively identify and challenge your own biases and those around you. Engage in difficult conversations with respect and openness. Commit to being an effective ally, focusing on meaningful inclusion rather than superficial gestures. In your professional environment, actively seek out and address biases, particularly in critical processes such as hiring and career advancement.

Chapter 8: Connecting with others

Cultivate meaningful connections by practising compassionate empathy, clarifying expectations, committing to each other, communicating effectively and creating sustaining rhythms and rituals.

Practise compassionate empathy by creating a safe space where other people feel heard, understood and not judged. Shift your focus from finding the perfect partner to becoming the right partner yourself. Work towards nurturing a thriving partnership. Begin by clearly understanding and communicating the expectations you and your partner have at different stages of your relationship. Commit to each other consistently, remembering this extends beyond exclusivity to prioritising your partner's needs and perspectives. Enhance your communication skills, employing tools such as love languages to deepen understanding. Finally, build a shared life by establishing and cherishing the rhythms and rituals that define your relationship.

Chapter 9: Working with others

Make the most of working with others by operating as an effective giver, fostering trust and psychological safety, contributing towards a shared purpose, set of values and behaviours, communicating effectively and operating within defined roles.

Enhance your collaboration skills by embodying the role of an effective giver. Practise expedition behaviour, balance your contributions and don't hesitate to seek help when needed. Recognise that team performance is a collective responsibility. Foster this by addressing three fundamental questions. Who are we as a team? How do we work together effectively? What are our current priorities? Work towards a unified understanding and articulation of these answers, ensuring each team member is aligned with the team's core purpose and values.

Chapter 10: Leading others

Lead others well by focusing on what you need to do rather than who you need to be, creating psychologically safe environments, setting high performance standards and engaging others on a rational and emotional level.

Embrace the practical aspects of managerial leadership by establishing clear performance standards, perhaps utilising the concept of a leader's intent for clarity and direction. Foster a psychologically safe environment where individuals can thrive by understanding their unique strengths and motivations. Apply a balanced leadership approach, working with a tight-loose-tight model, providing clear guidelines, allowing autonomy combined with clear accountability. Effectively lead change by valuing both emotional and rational perspectives and challenging the status quo of 'that's just how things are done'.

Final thought: over to you

I hope this book has not only been enjoyable and informative but also a practical guide to finding fulfilment. Whether it's building meaningful foundations, creating meaningful alignment or cultivating meaningful connections, my greatest hope is that you can integrate these lessons into your everyday life.

I'm eager to hear about your progress. Feel free to reach out to me at pete@mybetterhuman.com, get the latest updates on my website at mybetterhuman.com, or connect with me on LinkedIn or Instagram @mybetterhuman.

If this book has impacted you positively, I'd be grateful if you could share your experience and leave a review. Your support means everything.

References

Adams, L (2021) *HR Disrupted*. Practical Inspiration Publishing.

Alicke, M D & Govorun, O (2005) 'The better-than-average effect'. In Alicke, M D, Dunning, D A & Krueger, J I (eds) *The Self in Social Judgment*. Psychology Press.

Amaechi, J (2021) *The Promises of Giants*. Nicholas Brealey Publishing.

Ariely, D (2009) *Predictably Irrational*. Harper.

Asch, S E (1951) 'Effects of group pressure upon the modification and distortion of judgment'. In Guetzkow, H (ed.) *Groups, Leadership and Men*. Carnegie Press.

Atkinson, J W & Feather, N T (1974) A *Theory of Achievement Motivation*. Krieger Publishing Company.

Bartlett, S (2021) *Happy Sexy Millionaire*. Yellow Kite.

Bartlett, S (2022) 'Steven Bartlett: Learning Live, London', September 2022. URL: learning-live.com/steven-bartlett-recording-session

Bartlett, S (2023) *The Diary of a CEO*. Random House.

Baumlin, J (1987) 'Persuasion, Rogerian rhetoric, and imaginative play'. *Rhetoric Society Quarterly* 17(1).

BBC (2022) 'Harry Maguire's appeal over guilty verdict in Greek court to be heard in June'. BBC Sport, 31 July. URL: bbc.co.uk/sport/football/62371608

Beardmore, M (2023) 'James Ward-Prowse: Southampton captain says "slipping standards" led to Premier League relegation'. BBC Sport. URL: bbc.co.uk/sport/football/65585199

Beck, A T (1991) *Cognitive Therapy and the Emotional Disorders*. Penguin.

Bertrand, M & Mullainathan, S (2003) 'Are Emily and Greg more employable than Lakisha and Jamal? A field experiment on labor market discrimination'.

American Economic Review 94(4).

Brach, T (2013) *True Refuge*. Hay House UK.

Brickman, C, & Campbell, D T (1971) 'Hedonic relativism and planning the good society'. In Apley, M H (ed.), *Adaption Level Theory: A symposium*. Academic Press.

Brown, B (2010) *The Gifts of Imperfection*. Hazelden Publishing.

Brown, B (2015a) *Daring Greatly*. Penguin Life.

Brown, B (2015b) *Rising Strong*. Vermillion.

Brown, B (2018) *Dare to Lead*. Vermillion.

Brown, B (2021) *Atlas of the Heart*. Vermillion.

Buckingham, M (2005) *First, Break All the Rules*. Pocket Books.

Buckingham, M & Clifton, D O (2004) *Now, Discover Your Strengths*. Simon & Schuster UK.

Burns, D D (1980) *Feeling Good*. William Morrow Paperbacks.

Campaign to End Loneliness (2023) 'The State of Loneliness 2023'. URL: campaigntoendloneliness.org/wp-content/uploads/The-State-of-Loneliness-2023-ONS-data-on-loneliness-in-Britain.pdf

Carse, J (1986) *Finite and Infinite Games*. The Free Press.

Catmull, E (2014) *Creativity, Inc.* Bantam.

Celestine, N (2018) 'What is affective forecasting? A psychologist explains'. Positive Psychology. URL: positivepsychology.com/affective-forecasting

Chapman, G (1992) *The Five Love Languages*. Moody Publishers.

Chua, H F, Boland, E J & Nisbett, E R (2005) 'Cultural variation in eye movements during scene perception'. *Proceedings of the National Academy of Sciences* 102(35).

Clear, J (2018) *Atomic Habits*. Random House Business.

Cohen-Hatton, S & Honey, R (2015) 'Goal-oriented training affects decision-making processes in virtual and simulated fire and rescue environments'. *Journal of Experimental Psychology* 21(4).

Cohen-Hatton, S (2019) *The Heat of the Moment*. Doubleday.

Corporate Research Forum (2022) 'Making a paradigm shift in leadership development'. URL: crforum.co.uk/events/by-invitation-making-a-paradigm-shift-in-leadershipdevelopment

Covey, S R (2020) *The 7 Habits of Highly Effective People*. Simon & Schuster UK.

Coyle, D (2018) *The Culture Code*. Random House.

Crocker, J, Luhtanen, R K, Cooper, M L & Bouvrette, A (2003) 'Contingencies of self-worth in college students: theory and measurement'. *Journal of Personality and Social Psychology* 85(5).

Cross, K (1977) 'Not can, but *will* college teaching be improved?' *New Directions for Higher Education* 17.

David, S (2017a) 'The gift and power of emotional courage'. TEDWomen. URL: ted.com/talks/susan_david_the_gift_and_power_of_emotional_courage

David, S (2017b) *Emotional Agility*. Penguin.

DCMS (2018) 'A connected society: a strategy for tackling loneliness – laying the foundations for change'. UK Department for Digital, Culture, Media & Sport. URL: assets.publishing.service.gov.uk/media/5fb66cf98fa8f54aafb3c333/6.4882_DCMS_Loneliness_Strategy_web_Update_V2.pdf

DCMS (2023) 'Tackling Loneliness annual report March 2023: the fourth year'. UK Department for Digital, Culture, Media & Sport. URL: gov.uk/government/publications/loneliness-annual-report-the-fourth-year/tackling-loneliness-annual-report-march-2023-the-fourth-year

De Bono, E (1985) *Six Thinking Hats*. Penguin Life.

Duckworth, A (2016) *Grit*. Vermillion.

Dunning, D (2011) 'Chapter five – the Dunning–Kruger effect: on being ignorant of one's own ignorance'. *Advances in Experimental Social Psychology* 44.

Eastwood, O (2022) *Belonging*. Quercus.

Edmondson, A C (2018) *The Fearless Organisation*. Wiley.

Ellis, A (1991) 'The revised ABCs of rational-emotive therapy (RET)'. *Journal of Rational-Emotive & Cognitive-Behavior Therapy* 9(3).

Ericsson, K.A, Krampe, R T & Tesch-Römer, C (1993) 'The role of deliberate practice in the acquisition of expert performance'. *Psychological Review* 100(3).

Feldman Barrett, L (2018) *How Emotions are Made*. Pan.

Frankl, V (1959) *Man's Search for Meaning*. Beacon Press.

García, H & Miralles, F (2017) *Ikigai*. Hutchinson.

Gardner, H (1983) *Frames of Mind*. Basic Books.

Garrod, C (2023) *Conscious Inclusion: How to 'do' EDI, one decision at a time*. Practical Inspiration.

Gartner (2020) 'NEAR: a new model to manage remote employees'. Gartner. URL: gartner.com/en/ documents/3983557

Gladwell, M (2009) *Outliers*. Penguin.

Goldin, C & Rouse, C (1997) 'Orchestrating impartiality: the impact of "blind" auditions on female musicians'. *American Economic Review* 90(4).

Goleman, D (1998) *Working with Emotional Intelligence*. Bloomsbury Publishing.

Gollwitzer, P M (1999) 'Implementation intentions: strong effects of simple plans'. *American Psychologist* 54.

Gollwitzer, P M & Oettingen, G (1998) 'The emergence and implementation of health goals'. *Psychology & Health* 13(4).

Gottman, J & Silver, N (1999) *The Seven Principles for Making Marriage Work*. Orion Spring.

Grant, A (2014) *Give and Take*. W&N.

Grant, A (2017) *Originals*. WH Allen.

Grant, A (Mar 2018) 'How to love criticism'. *WorkLife with Adam Grant*. URL: ted.com/talks/worklife_with_ adam_grant_how_to_love_criticism

Grant, A (Mar 2020) 'Burnout is Everyone's Problem'. *WorkLife with Adam Grant*. URL: ted.com/talks/

worklife_with_adam_grant_burnout_is_everyone_s_problem

Grant, A (Apr 2020a) 'Authenticity is a double-edged sword'. *Worklife with Adam Grant*, 7 April. URL: ted.com/talks/worklife_with_adam_grant_authenticity_is_a_double_edged_sword

Grant, A (Apr 2020b) 'Reinventing the job interview'. *WorkLife with Adam Grant*. URL: ted.com/talks/worklife_with_adam_grant_reinventing_the_job_interview

Grant, A (May 2021) 'Who's the boss?' *WorkLife with Adam Grant*. URL: ted.com/talks/worklife_with_adam_grant_who_s_the_boss

Grant, A (May 2022) 'Breaking up with perfectionism'. *Worklife with Adam Grant*. URL: ted.com/talks/worklife_with_adam_grant_breaking_up_with_perfectionism

Grant, A (Oct 2022) 'Malcolm Gladwell experiments with Adam's class'. *WorkLife with Adam Grant*. URL: open.spotify.com/episode/0yzwg58XBoVF75lzRjVtg8

Groeschel, C (2018) 'Six types of leaders: Part 1'. *Craig Groeschel Leadership Podcast*. URL: life.church/leadershippodcast/six-types-of-leaders-part-1

Guthridge, L (2018) 'How to Drive Success With Three Little Words'. *Forbes*. URL: forbes.com/sites/forbescoachescouncil/2018/08/10/how-to-drive-success-with-three-little-words

Harari, D, Swider, B W, Steed, L B & Breidenthal, A P (2018) 'Is perfect good? A meta-analysis of perfectionism in the workplace'. *Journal of Applied Psychology* 103(10).

Hartling, L M, Rosen, W, Walker, M & Jordan, J V (2000) 'Shame and humiliation: from isolation to relational transformation. Work in progress'. URL: humiliation-studies.org/documents/hartling/HartlingShameHumiliation.pdf

Heath, C & Heath, D (2010) *Switch*. Random House Business.

Heath, C & Heath, D (2014) *Decisive*. Random House Business.

Heen, S & Stone, D (2014) 'Find the coaching in criticism'. *Harvard Business Review*. URL: hbr.org/2014/01/find-the-coaching-in-criticism

Huckman, R S & Pisano, G P (2006) 'The firm specificity of individual performance: evidence from cardiac surgery'. *Management Science* 52(4).

Humphrey, J & Hughes, D (Apr 2020) 'Holly Tucker: Wait for the right time and you'll wait forever' (No 8). *The High Performance Podcast*. URL: thehighperformancepodcast.com/podcast/holly-tucker

Humphrey, J, & Hughes, D (Sep 2020) 'Jonny Wilkinson: how a mental health crisis led to a life of exploration' (No 23). *The High Performance Podcast*, 21 September. URL: thehighperformancepodcast.com/podcast/jonny-wilkinson

Humphrey, J & Hughes, D (Nov 2020). 'Billy Monger: It's not the fact but how you react' (No 29). *The High Performance Podcast*, 23 November. URL: thehighperformancepodcast.com/podcast/billy-monger

Humphrey, J & Hughes, D (Jul 2021) 'Mel Marshall: The art and science of great coaching' (No 74). *The High Performance Podcast*. URL: thehighperformancepodcast.com/podcast/melmarshall

Humphrey, J & Hughes, D (Apr 2022) 'Lewis Morgan: How I made £100m in 8 years and learned there is no secret' (No 115). *The High Performance Podcast*, 18 April. URL: thehighperformancepodcast.com/podcast/lewismorgan

Humphrey, J & Hughes, D (Dec 2022) 'Adam Grant: Why you should stop trying to prove yourself and start trying to improve yourself' (No 164). *The High Performance Podcast*. URL: thehighperformancepodcast.com/podcast/adamgrant

Humphrey, J & Hughes, D (2023) *High Performance*. Penguin.

Iger, R (2019) *The Ride of a Lifetime*. Transworld Digital.

Jachimowicz, J M (2019) '3 reasons it's so hard to 'follow your passion''. *Harvard Business Review*. URL: hbr.org/2019/10/3-reasons-its-so-hard-to-follow-your-passion

Kahn, W A (1990) 'Psychological conditions of personal engagement and disengagement at work'. *Academy of Management Journal* 33.

Kahneman, D (2012) *Thinking, Fast and Slow*. Penguin.

Kegan, R & Lahey, L (2009) *Immunity to Change*. Harvard Business Review Press.

Keller, M & Meaney, M (2017) *Leading Organizations*. Bloomsbury Business.

Kerr, J (2013) *Legacy*. Constable.

Klein, G (2007). 'Performing a project premortem'. *Harvard Business Review*. URL: hbr.org/2007/09/performing-a-project-premortem

Klein, N (1999) *Time to Think*. Octopus.

Kotter, J (2012) *Leading Change*. Harvard Business Review Press.

Lencioni, P (2002) *The Five Dysfunctions of a Team*. John Wiley & Sons.

Leslie, I (2022) *How to Disagree*. Faber & Faber.

Lewis, M (2012) 'Obama's way'. *Vanity Fair*, October. URL: vanityfair.com/news/2012/10/michael-lewis-profile-barack-obama

Mahdawi, A (2022) *Strong Female Lead*. Coronet.

Marquet, D (2013) *Turn the Ship Around*. Portfolio Penguin.

Maslow, A H (1943) 'A theory of human motivation'. *Psychological Review* 50(4).

Maxwell, J (2007) *Talent is Never Enough*. Nelson Bibles.

Merton, R K (1968) 'The Matthew effect in science'. *Science* 159(3810).

Milano A (2017) 'If you've been sexually harassed or assaulted, write "me too" as a reply to this tweet.' Twitter/X, 15 October. URL: researchgate.net/

figure/Tweet-of-Alyssa-Milano-October-15-2017_
fig1_332923950

Milkman, K L, Beshears, J et al (2011) 'Using implementation
intention prompts to enhance influenza vaccination
rates'. *Proceedings of the National Academy of Sciences*
108(26).

MOD (2022) 'Psychological Safety in MOD major projects'.
UK Ministry of Defence. URL: gov.uk/government/
publications/psychological-safety-in-mod-major-
projects

Murphy, K (2020) *You're Not Listening*. Random House.

NBA Europe (2023) 'There is no failure in sports'. URL:
youtube.com/watch?v=9mXGSjnUvSM

New Living Translation Bible (2015) Tyndale House
Publishers. URL: biblegateway.com/versions/New-
Living-Translation-NLT-Bible

Nickerson, D W & Rogers, T (2010) 'Do you have a voting
plan? Implementation intentions, voter turnout, and
organic plan making'. *Psychological Science* 21(2).

Nisbett, R & Masuda, T (2003) 'Culture and point of view'.
Proceedings of the National Academy of Sciences 100(10).

Nouwen, H J (2004) *Out of Solitude*. Ave Maria Press.

O'Keefe, P A, Dweck, C S & Walton, G M (2018) 'Implicit
theories of interest: finding your passion or developing
It?' *Psychological Science*, 29(10).

Pattakos, A & Covey, S R (2010) *Prisoners of Our Thoughts*.
Berrett-Koehler Publishers.

Pennebaker, J W (2004) *Writing to Heal*. Center for Journal
Therapy.

Pink, D (2018) *Drive*. Canongate Books

Purja, N (2020) *Beyond Possible*. Hodder Paperbacks.

Randolph, M (2021) *That Will Never Work*. Endeavour.

Richardson-Walsh, H & Richardson-Walsh, K (2021)
Winning Together. Nicholas Brealey Publishing.

Rodriguez, D (2015) 'Hiring: it's about cultural contribution,
not cultural fit. LinkedIn, 10 September. URL: linkedin.

com/pulse/how-i-hire-its-all-cultural-contribution-fit-diego-rodriguez

Roosevelt, T (1910) 'Citizenship in a republic'. Address at the Sorbonne in Paris, France.

Ross, W (2006) 'What is REBT?' URL: rebtnetwork.org/whatis.html

Rotter, J B (1966) 'Generalized expectancies for internal versus external control of reinforcement'. *Psychological Monographs: General and Applied* 80(1).

Salovey, P & Mayer, J D (1990) 'Emotional intelligence'. *Imagination, Cognition, and Personality*, 9(3).

Sandberg, S & Grant, A (2019) *Option B*. WH Allen.

Scott, K (2019) *Radical Candor*. Pan.

Scott, K (2022) *Just Work*. Pan.

Scott, K (2023) '11 tactical tips for getting feedback from others'. Radical Candor. URL: radicalcandor.com/blog/get-feedback

Seligman, M (1972) 'Learned helplessness'. *Annual review of medicine*, 23(1).

Seligman, M (2006) *Learned Optimism*. Vintage.

Sinek, S (2011) *Start with Why*. Penguin.

Sinek, S (2014) *Leaders Eat Last*. Penguin.

Sinek, S (2019) *The Infinite Game*. Penguin.

Sinek, S (2023). Twitter, 7 June. Retrieved 9 June 2023, from @simonsinek.

Stone, D, Patton, B & Heen, S (2010) *Difficult Conversations*. Penguin.

Sutton, R (2010) *The No Asshole Rule*. Business Plus.

Svenson, O (1981) 'Are we all less risky and more skilful than our fellow drivers?' Acta Psychologica 47(2).

Syed, M (2011) *Bounce*. Fourth Estate.

Syed, M (2015) *Black Box Thinking*. Penguin.

Syed, M (2019) *Rebel Ideas*. John Murray Publishers.

Tannenbaum, S & Salas, E (2023) *Teams that Work*. OUP USA.

Tewfik, B A (2022) 'The impostor phenomenon

revisited: examining the relationship between workplace impostor thoughts and interpersonal effectiveness at work'. *Academy of Management Journal* 65(3).

Thaler, R & Sunstein, Cass R (2022) *Nudge*. Penguin.

Traumatic Stress Institute (2007) 'Shame and attachment'. URL: traumaticstressinstitute.org/wp-content/files_mf/1276631745ShameandAttachment.pdf

Trusted Advisor Associates (nd) 'Understanding the trust equation'. Trusted Advisor. URL: trustedadvisor.com/why-trust-matters/understanding-trust/understanding-the-trust-equation

Tupper, H & Ellis, S (2020) *The Squiggly Career*. Penguin.

Urban, T (2014) '10 types of odd friendships you're probably part of'. Wait But Why. URL: waitbutwhy.com/2014/12/10-types-odd-friendships-youre-probably-part

Voss, C & Raz, T (2017) *Never Split the Difference*. Random House Business.

Waldinger, R (November 2015) 'What makes a good life? Lessons from the longest study on happiness'. TEDxBeaconStreet. URL: ted.com/talks/robert_waldinger_what_makes_a_good_life_lessons_from_the_longest_study_on_happiness

Whyte, G (1986) 'Escalating commitment to a course of action: a reinterpretation'. *The Academy of Management Review* 11(2).

Wiseman, T (1996) 'A concept analysis of empathy'. *Journal of Advanced Nursing* 23(6).

World Health Organization (2006) 'Constitution of the World Health Organization – basic documents, forty-fifth edition, supplement'.

Wright, H N (2004) *101 Questions to Ask Before You Get Engaged*. Harvest House Publishers.

Young, V (2011) *The Secret Thoughts of Successful Women*. Crown Publishing Group.

Online resources

Amazing If Free Squiggly Careers Toolkit: amazingif.com/toolkit

Atomic Habits resources'. URL: jamesclear.com/atomic-habits/resources

CliftonStrengths assessment: gallup.com/cliftonstrengths

Cognitive Bias Codex: commons.wikimedia.org/wiki/File:Cognitive_bias_codex_en.svg

Find Your WHY course, The Optimism Company: simonsinek.com/product/find-your-why-with-simon

The High Performance Podcast: thehighperformancepodcast.com

Insights Discovery: insights.com/products/insights-discovery

MBA Oath: mbaoath.org/take-the-mba-oath

MindTools (Locus of control, the Situation-Behavior-Impact™ Feedback Tool and other resources): mindtools.com

Strengthscope: strengthscope.com

Acknowledgements

I'd like to thank those whose contributions to my pursuit towards becoming a better human inspired this book. It's impossible to distill a lifetime of advice, research and reading into a brief section, and I owe a debt of gratitude to every author, thought leader and podcaster referenced in this book, especially those listed in the 'Go Deeper' sections. However, I do want to specifically call out a few individuals.

First, Professor Damian Hughes, for not only the wisdom you've shared through your books and podcasts but also the feedback you provided in the early stages of the writing process. As a first-time author, your encouragement gave me the belief to continue with the project.

Leah, thank you for being with me the whole way, reading every chapter and sharing how, even in its early drafts, this book was making a difference. Knowing that kept me writing, even in the hardest moments.

Roger, you continue to be a great mentor, and your advice and guidance are invaluable and something I truly treasure.

I also want to thank every single person who has read and given me feedback on the chapters of this book. Simeon, Becky, James, Heather, Mum, Jess – without all of you, there would be no book.

I am deeply grateful to those who have read the book and are prepared to endorse it. Thank you, Caroline, Nick, Amber and Catherine.

I wouldn't have got here without the unwavering support of my wife, Becky. Thank you for always supporting me and helping me see this through to completion.

Finally, making this dream a reality has been an incredibly exciting process, and I'd like to thank my publishing team at the Right Book Company for being such a pleasure to work with. Thank you, Sue, Beverley, Paul, Andrew and Nick.